MAKING

ROOM FOR

GD

anne slamkowski

Revealing Faith

LEARNING HOW TO
PLACE GOD FIRST
IN YOUR LIFE

anne slamkowski

Revealing Faith

LEARNING HOW TO PLACE
GOD FIRST IN YOUR LIFE

First edition published 2012
Green Olive Books

Library of Congress Control Number: 2012947432

Interior and Cover Design: Lindsay Hadley

To the women in my life that constantly inspire me. Robin, Genny, Emily, Tami, Jan and Jenny you continually remind me of the importance of placing God first in my life. Our weekly meetings are the joy of my week!

To my ultimate inspiration – my family. Pete you are my rock and my reminder that God loves me unconditionally. Megan, TJ and Kate you are the strength behind this book. I am thankful for my little cheerleaders!

TABLE
OF CONTENTS

PLACING

G*Introduction*D

FIRST IN MY LIFE

It was a beautiful Thanksgiving Day. After flying six hours with three kids, Pete and I were exhausted. Nevertheless, life seemed good. We were completely surrounded by family, and the love in the room could build mountains. There was so much food. The smell permeated my sister Jenny's entire house. It wasn't often that we were able to spend time with family. After all we lived 1500 miles from family in the mountains of Northern Utah. Our small community was encased within a valley area which housed a total of 100,000 people. Every day we would wake up to fresh, crisp mountain air surrounded by mountain scenery and mule deer trotting down the very street on which we drove. For two years we had resided quite far away from family, so we were excited to be with them on this Thanksgiving Day in 2005. It was almost one year to the day since we had given birth to our daughter Kate. Kate was such a blessing to Pete and me, since we had been without an infant for several years. Our two older children Megan and TJ were five and six when Kate was born. As we celebrated Thanksgiving, we also thanked God for the special gift of Kate one year before.

Kate was a happy child who just melted with excitement at all the new faces of her family. Of course my family just hugged and kissed on her all day. After a long day of gluttony and football, we headed back to my mom's house to collapse for the night. Pete and I noticed that Kate had been coughing most of the day. She seemed fever free, but certainly she didn't sound well. As experienced parents, we divided up the night into shifts so we both could get at least a little sleep that evening. Pete took the first shift, and around two in the morning he awoke me with a very ill child. Pete's frightened eyes clued me in that something was seriously wrong.

Jumping out of bed, I saw Kate in Pete's arms convulsing on one side of her body. I immediately thought seizure when I saw her. I am still not sure why; I wasn't familiar with seizures. A few months back, we had been at a Notre Dame Football game and attended Mass afterward. During that Mass, with thousands of people surrounding us, a young man had a seizure. He was immediately pulled out into the aisle, and people started to work on him. I found it very frightening and began to pray for him instantly. However, this time Kate was even more difficult to watch. She was vomiting out the side of her mouth, and her small body seemed so fragile and weak. I screamed for my mom to call 911. My sister and brother were both at the house with us and they came down to help. My sister took over the 911 call because the ambulance was having difficulty finding my mom's house. Kate had been seizing for over 25 minutes at this point. My mom and I held hands and prayed. I cannot tell you exactly what we prayed for. My mind was scrolling through the "what ifs" at that point. What if they don't get here, what if she dies, what if she is terminally ill, and what will I tell the kids? Confusion and loss of control overwhelmed me as I realized, "I don't have control – and really never did to begin with."

God had the wheel, and I wasn't sure where He was taking us or what direction we were heading. Thank goodness for my mom that night who could pray the words that I couldn't form in my mind. She prayed for the ambulance, for Kate's health and for strength for our family. At the hospital, Kate had to endure a spinal tap, which my brother and Pete had to witness. After the spinal tap, my sisters and I went into the ER and saw tears in both my brother and Pete's eyes. The depth of what they had just witnessed touched my heart. I was blessed to have their strength that night – the strength that I could not even begin to regain until I let go of the anxiety that I had from loss of control. God was definitely present in this hospital. There was no doubt in my mind. Once meningitis was ruled out, the doctors assumed the seizure was febrile (fever induced seizures). My mother's instinct (which I like to call the Holy Spirit working within me) told me this was not quite right. It was like a red light flashing brightly in the room that for some reason I could only see. I knew there was more to this, but in my mind, I just needed to get back to Utah and figure it all out.

After returning to Utah, it took months of doctor visits and constantly advocating for my child before I would get a referral to a neurologist in Salt Lake City. Eventually, after many, many seizure episodes, Kate would be diagnosed with complex partial seizures. This is really a complicated word for seizures that happen but usually go unnoticed. Kate only had convulsions the one night we went by ambulance to the ER. Mostly, her seizures looked like blank stares, purple lips, and loss of breath with extreme exhaustion. This was the beginning of a very long learning process for both Pete and me. It would take years for us to find the right medication for Kate; not only keeping the seizures controlled, but controlling behavioral issues, ADHD, anxiety and depressive disorder. All of this tested the patience that God had given me and caused me to ask, "Are you sure I am the right person for this child?" Still, I knew that He is always putting the right people in my life who show me ways to parent with patience. One thing I have learned through all of this is God does not call us because we are worthy. He makes us worthy.

So what does all this have to do with Revealing Faith? This situation is only "doable" because of God. It is through His strength that Pete and I are able to parent effectively and lovingly. It took us months, maybe even years to be revealed. I probably would have suffered under the palm of my own control issues. I probably would have lost patience with the other two precious children he gave to me. I probably would have lost the relationship with my husband.

I COR 12:26-27 "If one part suffers, all the parts suffer with it; if one part is honored all the parts share its joy. Now you are Christ's body and individually parts of it."

If I had chosen to wallow in misery, then my entire family would have been right there suffering with me. I knew I had to pull myself together and move forward with God's help. God is so great at waiting until we ask Him for help. He truly waits until we are ready. Now that doesn't mean I don't think He ever nudges me first. He does, but sometimes I just am not listening. I try to focus on His call, but sometimes I need a sledgehammer, not just a tap on the back. God was not punishing our family with these seizures. He was blessing us with a struggle so we could become closer to the love He so desperately wanted to share with us. Once I finally let myself see this, I began to trust again.

2 TIM 2:3 "Bear Your share of the hardship along with me like a good soldier of Christ Jesus."

God knew the Slamkowski's could handle this. He entrusted us with this precious child and with this struggle. After all, Kate is first a child of God. He is just allowing Pete and me the ability to teach her the faith. How awesome is that!

By blessing us with this seemingly unbearable event, God showed me that His strength is all I need. Because of this, I began to pen this book, so that I could share God's grace with all who read it.

Capturing the spirit of your own faith can be difficult in today's world. Worldliness, busyness, and evil can divert your attention from God and place it on fear, boredom, anger, and envy. While writing this book, I found that my own discomfort helped me to discover more ways that I have pushed God out of my own life. I am hopeful that just like me, you will be able to uncover those uncomfortable feelings and discover the benefit of placing God first.

"You don't asphalt the road of life, but you put guardrails along the cliff."
—EXCERPT FROM "GOD IS NO STRANGER"

CHAPTER
ONE

HANDLING LIFE'S STRUGGLES

Now that I have completely thrown you into the circle of my life, I should explain a little about my family's background. My husband, Pete, and I have three beautiful children whom God entrusted to us. Pete and I were what some would call a "mixed marriage." I was raised in the United Methodist Church and Pete was reared Catholic. I should probably add here Polish Catholic because that seemed to be quite important later on in our marriage. Pete said his grandmother always told him to find a good Polish Catholic girl to marry. He says he got two of the four, good and girl. That might be a little debatable too! We were taught through our marriage preparation classes that religion was the most important factor in our marriage. This fact would be strengthened every year we were married. Truly, when you think about the sacrament of marriage – the union is between God, Pete, and me. After all, to leave God out of this equation would be a big mistake. Who else can explain unconditional love and model it so beautifully?

COL 3:12-14 "Put on then, as God's chosen ones, holy and beloved, heartfelt compassion, kindness, humility, gentleness, and patience, bearing with one another and forgiving one another, if one has a grievance against another; as the Lord has forgiven you, so must you also do. And over all these put on love, that is, the bond of perfection."

When Jesus modeled love it was amazing. His faith in people even those who would deceive him were unimaginable. I mean when people cross the line of friendship with me, I have a hard time inviting them back into my life. I am lacking this true testament of unconditional love. Even when I read scriptures over and over each Sunday at Mass, I cannot help but think, "How in the world can I possibly be like Christ?" I constantly doubt others and worry about life and gossip. Why has God entrusted me with this great family when I am obviously such a poor role model and sinner? This is usually when Pete chimes in with how much I have changed his life and how he was inspired to be a bigger part of the church because of my own service to God. Just like that Colossians verse – we inspire and forgive each other without even realizing it because God calls us to do so. The best part is Pete has done the same for me.

The "Imitation of Christ" has a wonderful section called "Following Christ our Model" Keep these four thoughts in mind:

- Christ's teaching surpasses that of all
- Have humility, know your limitations
- Don't put your trust in riches
- Center Your love on what is unseen not seen

All of this certainly begs the question – Was my faith always like this? Faith has been instilled in me for most of my life. In fact as far back as I can remember, my parents were a driving force of my Methodist upbringing. There were many days when my mom toted me along to her volunteer projects. After all, I am the youngest of five, and at that point my mom was more than willing to escape the house with a toddler in tow. Those first children we hold so close to us – keeping them clear of illness and other people. We certainly wouldn't want them to get sick or be touched too much – it might over stimulate them! By the time a mother gives birth to number five, she is more relaxed and accepting of the outside world. Because of that, I experienced my mom's giving back to God on a regular basis. My parents both took mission trips to Liberia Africa to help rebuild a school and church. God gave them all they had, and they were devoted enough to give Him back those gifts and more. My Sundays were filled with worship, potlucks, Sunday Schools, and youth group. It was a blessing.

When I started college, my life fell away from God. Self-esteem can be one of our biggest enemies and causes of our own sinful behavior. Don't ever doubt that the devil will use that whenever he can. My low self-esteem certainly eased my way down a life of hardship. One recommendation as a parent is to give our children the tools needed for better self-esteem.

Recently, one of Kate's doctors recommended a book on HSC (highly sensitive children). In this book, there is a wonderful section on promoting self-esteem in children. *The Highly Sensitive Child*, by Elaine N. Aron, Ph.D. gives these following six pointers:

1. Look at yourself.
   Your actions, posture, tone of voice and facial expressions speak louder than words to your kids.
2. Words Count, too. Find words that speak proudly of your children instead of criticizing them for their faults.
3. Spend time with your child. Nothing says "I like you" like wanting to be with someone.
4. Show respect. Use your words to show that your child's feelings, needs, opinions preferences and decisions all are valid emotions. It may not be the best emotion, but it is valid.
5. Help your child understand himself in relation to other people. Teach your child to acknowledge other's feelings, and try to think more deeply about what causes people to act in a certain way. Dr Aron even suggests saying for example, "I wonder if he was just in a bad mood – you know how you can sometimes say things you don't mean."
6. Bring up strengths when your child mentions a weakness. Honor the child's feeling, but add to it showing them the strength that may be hidden to their own eyes.

Dr. Aron's book is definitely centered on the "Highly Sensitive Child" which would be the definition of my Kate, but it can be used for all children. It is just a different view of parenting kids that maybe need that extraordinary parent.

One of the best bible verses for parenting is in the book of Proverbs.

PROVERBS 22:6 "Train up a child in the way he should go, even when he is old he will not depart from it."

That speaks volumes about what God wants us to do as parents. In today's world our children are so over stimulated and instantly gratified that they never have a chance to experience the beauty of what God has created. More importantly, they never experience failure and prayer is nonexistent in many households.

After school, I can vividly remember going outside to play with my friends. Homework was rare and life was enjoyed by all of us. The natural terrain of my neighborhood provided us with intense imaginary games and stories. Sometimes springtime smells permeate the air, and it takes me back to those freeing moments of playtime. Life was peaceful and filled with the nature that God created for us. My parents saw the importance of spending time with friends and enjoying the outdoors because we didn't have all the electronics and cable programs of today. It might have been an easier time to parent, but the morals that my parents instilled in me are what make me who I am today. My parents allowed me to make mistakes, which made me stronger. They embedded on my soul that God was with me, and he would give me the strength to overcome any of my weaknesses.

As I have stated, my life in college definitely made me lean back on those values that my parents had taught me. Allowing me to make mistakes would come in handy later in life, as I had to get myself out of the holes I had dug. I cannot explain why I chose that lowly path. I knew the way back to the high road; I just wasn't ready to take it. My parents had shown me the path home, very clearly. It would take time for me to realize that God would forgive me, and I could move forward. Bad choices are always a focus when I look back. Why on earth did I make choices that made my life so difficult? Even through those years, I can manage to see God's light, and I am thankful that he saw good in those bad circumstances.

In **MATTHEW 7:24-25**, the bible tells us "Everyone who listens to these words of mine and acts on them will be like a wise man who built his house on rock. The rain fell, the floods came, and the winds blew and buffeted the house. But it did not collapse; it had been set solidly on rock."

Thankfully, my background was set up on rock. Parenting, with God at the center, was my mom and dad's strong point. They knew the importance of scripture, church based friendships, communities centered upon God, and giving back to God in many forms. There was never a doubt in my mind, even when I stumbled, that God was with me. This is not to say that if your life was built on sand that you have no chance. It just may be a bigger battle than I encountered. Anything is possible with God. My mom mentioned to me one day that we are so fortunate that our houses here in Indiana are set on such hard clay dirt. Think of those homes in Florida that are built on sand. Thinking back on our conversation, I cannot help but wonder if it really matters what your house is built on. Somehow even through the most tumultuous storms, the Florida homes still exist. I realize that some Florida homes may fall during storms, but some homes in Indiana fall during tough tornado winds. Even the solid rock foundation can falter if you don't keep God first in your life. My parents gave me the right tools; it was within my free will to use this gift of God correctly. I definitely struggled with it, but I finally lassoed it in.

At the age of 23, I met my match. Pete Slamkowski would remind me the importance of Christ in my life. This great man that God introduced me to while jogging would change my life forever. With a little encouragement, I went back to church and began going to bible study. My mom fortunately had a bible study that met weekly at her house. After the first meeting, I was hooked. The spiritual uplift that I received by reading God's word was unexplainable. God was working hard on me, and I was thrilled with the change. I wasn't perfect, but this change was evident in my life.

Engagement came in the form of my mother's wedding ring at my parent's lake cabin in Southern Indiana. Two weeks after Pete asked me to marry him; he was transferred to Illinois. I could handle two hours from my home in Indiana. Life was going to be good – I just needed to trust in God's plan. I would stay in Indiana for a year while planning our wedding and Pete would live in Illinois. After we were married, I moved over to Illinois with Pete. This was the first test of our marriage. As a Methodist, I was searching for that perfect church community, and as a Catholic, Pete started right in attending the closest church for Mass. It was natural for him to just go to Mass and then be finished with his Sunday obligation. That was not the case for me. I was searching for bible studies, worship service, fellowship, ministries and all other aspects of the church that I grew up knowing. This was proving to be difficult, tedious and lonely.

My faith suffered, and so did our marriage. A year later, still with no home base, I was lost. I threw myself into work and school (I was going back to college for my second degree in Education). Somehow this wasn't settling right either. It was complicated and sad. God seemed to have taken a backseat in my life. I dove into anything I could just to escape the unhappiness and loneliness that I was feeling inside. Isn't it funny how we try to busy ourselves with "stuff" just so we don't have to think about how far we pushed God out of our lives?

When I think of how isolated I felt, I couldn't help but think of the apostle Paul. Paul sat in jail for many years. Some of his best evangelization was done from that jail cell. You see Paul was a Roman Jew that converted to "the Way." He was incarcerated for this when the authorities finally caught up with him evangelizing for Jesus. That didn't stop Paul. He continued his work writing all the people whom he had visited. In fact, the letter to the Galatians sticks in my mind the most. The Galatians are just like I am. When Paul was there, they were on a high for Jesus. They couldn't get enough of it! The minute Paul left, those Galatians turned right back to their old ways.

In **GALATIANS 3:1** Paul starts out by saying "O you stupid Galatians! Who has bewitched you, before whose eyes Jesus Christ was publicly portrayed as crucified."

Each week, I go to church and hear a great sermon on the scriptures. Walking out, I am energized by those words of God. I seem armed and ready for battle, but the minute I walk out that door, something happens. I allow the world to take over. I forget God is there. Loneliness sets in all over again. Incarceration certainly didn't stop Paul from writing those harsh words that needed to be uttered. You would think that Paul would have been depressed, lonely and ready to give up the fight. Just the contrary, he fought from the isolation. He battled through the depression. He remembered that God was with him – Paul was not alone.

The imminent conclusion seemed to be that converting to Catholicism might be a less lonely option. Whether that was the right reason to convert, it was how I came to know the Catholic faith. Sometimes, we don't do things for the right reasons, but God uses this for His good. Thank goodness he sees the good in it because there were many times in my life that my path became tangled, but God seemed to know how to unknot it quite well. What I found during this year long conversion process was that it brought Pete and me very close. We were learning the faith together. The Catholic Church does a fabulous job teaching the faith. In a series of weekly meetings, for a year, one learns all about the church and what it means to be Catholic. All of this ends with the liturgy on Holy Saturday (the Saturday before Easter Sunday) at what is called the Easter Vigil. It is a beautiful service that centers upon the resurrection of our Lord and is a reminder that there is a "new life" in Christ. After this wonderful rebirth of my faith, Pete and I found the importance of faith once again in our lives.

In the next several years, we would lose my father to a heart attack and give birth to two beautiful children. Life is a roller coaster ride, but God is holding the wheel and that is all I need to know and trust. As it happens to be in life, just when things seemed perfect and in place, Pete came home to talk to me at lunchtime. Let me put it this way: Pete worked fifteen minutes from our home and NEVER came home for lunch. My alarms were going off like crazy. His company wanted to transfer him to Northern Utah. The job would begin in two months. I never doubted for a moment that we should go. In fact there was a sense of peace that could not be shaken from within me. Holy Spirit there you are!

Our Illinois house sold by word of mouth to a friend, and we bought a home in a small community in Utah, population 9800. It was a beautiful God-filled community. Maybe it was the majestic mountains that surrounded our house or just that God made his presence known so clearly through the people, but life in Utah was unshakably God-filled. Our church was small, but warm and loving. It was a circle of people who trusted in God's plan. Our friendships were based on Christ, and meals with our friends started with prayer. Bible studies, Sunday school, and coffee with friends enriched our faith naturally and fulfilled our marriage. Struggles were encountered with gratitude and trust in God's plan. It was a daily occurrence to ask someone to pray for us. Life was pure and simple – it was peaceful. God's beauty of creation was eye opening. The glorious hikes we would take as a family on Sundays or maybe just hop over to the mom and pop ski resort through the canyon were plentiful. God came first, then family second. Our faith took an astonishing leap in Utah because we were able to put God first so easily.

I can remember exactly where I was when Pete came home that sunny September day in 2006. I was sitting in our front parlor room piecing together a quilt that I was making with scraps. My mom was visiting us, and she was napping with Kate. Pete came home for lunch and once again this was an odd occurrence. Again, I knew the minute he wandered in what he was going to say. Excitement was bubbling within me. Thinking deeply about where God was going to move us this time, I said, "Is it somewhere good – like the Midwest?" Pete can never just say yes or no! He, like a woman, likes to go through all the details of the transfer. His words trailed off, "So and so called me…blah blah blah…"

At least that is what in my mind registered until I heard "…to the Midwest." Praise God!!! We are going home. I could hardly wait to go wake my mom. I yelled, "Mom, we are coming home! " My mom and I were ready to pack up that minute. Unfortunately, corporate America doesn't move quite that fast, but I do. One month later we were sitting in my mom's family room for good. God had brought us full circle, and new life was born again within the Slamkowski household.

Study Questions

● **INTRODUCTION AND CHAPTER ONE**

01

Was there one instance or many instances that you can recall that made you realize something was missing in your life?

02

When you had a "stumbling block" or struggle in your life how did you handle it?

03

I COR 12:26-27 "If one part suffers, all the parts suffer with it; if one part is honored all the parts share its joy. Now you are Christ's body and individually parts of it."

Can you think of a time that you struggled through a trial, and you took your family, friends or church members down with you? What could you have done differently so that all parts didn't need to suffer?

04

Read **COLOSSIANS 3:12-14**. Was there a time in your life that you found it hard to forgive someone? What steps did you take to truly forgive that person?

05

Reflect on the Imitation of Christ, Following Christ Our Model on page 8. What does that mean to you personally? How do you follow that Model, and where in your life do you fail to follow that model?

06

Read **MATTHEW 7:24-25**. What is your foundation in faith? Is it rock solid or built on sand? How does that formation of faith help you today? If yours was built on sand – how can you change that to rock?

07

The Apostle Paul sat in jail for years writing letters to the people in the outside world. Have you ever felt lonely or depressed in life before? What can you use to fill the void of loneliness? How can you, like Paul, use bad circumstances for the good of God?

08

Finding a "new life" in Christ was an important part of my faith life. Think about the times in your life that you have been able to start again and refocus on what is important. Read **ROMANS 6:3-5** to help you better understand this concept of new life.

CHAPTER
TWO

INCREASING YOUR TIME WITH GOD

Where on earth did this notion of placing God first in our life come from?

MATTHEW 6:33 But seek first the kingdom of God and his righteousness, and all these things will be added to you.

MATTHEW 6:24 No one can serve two masters, for either he will hate the one and love the other, or he will be devoted to the one and despise the other. You cannot serve God and money.

2 CORINTHIANS 8:5 And this, not as we expected, but they gave themselves first to the Lord and then by the will of God to us

JOHN 3:30 He must increase, I must decrease.

Getting our faith in check requires a person to place God first. I have found this to be such a struggle in life because everyday options take me away from God. During a normal day of my life, I probably put God on the backburner several times. If only I could realize that I am doing this. God should be constantly on the forefront of my life; it would be so much easier if I just appreciated this. Currently, I work at our church about twenty hours a week. I enjoy my time there immensely because I am immersed in things that are Godly. You would think that my choices would constantly be Christ centered. A 24-hour Adoration chapel exists right in our church, which at any time I could walk up to, and pray for God to help me with difficult decisions. In my two years working at the church, I have done that maybe twice during my work hours. Why can't I seem to place God first?

A conversation with God just seems uncomfortable sometimes. Here is the number one clue that you are not placing God first in your life –**prayer is not present within your home, work and church life.** If I never spoke to Pete or my kids, if I just woke up in the morning and went about my day without speaking or acknowledging them – how do you think they would feel? I can guarantee you – they would not feel loved. If we do not take time to converse with God, we are not showing him the love that he so desires and deserves from us.

Max Lucado's book *Grace for the Moment* speaks volumes on the importance of prayer. In the section "*Prayers Make a Difference*" he says, "Most of our prayer lives could use a tune-up. Some prayer lives lack consistency. They're either a desert or an oasis. Long, arid, dry spells interrupted by brief plunges into the waters of communion…Others of us need sincerity. Our prayers are a bit hollow, memorized and rigid; more liturgy than life. And though they are daily, they are dull. Still others lack, well, honesty. We honestly wonder if prayer makes a difference. Why on earth would God in heaven want to talk to me? If God knows all, who am I to tell him anything? If God controls all, who am I to do anything? Our prayers may be awkward. Our attempts may be feeble. But since the power of prayer is in the one who hears it and not the one who says it, our prayers do make a difference."

God desires a relationship with us, but in order for us to do that – we must pray. Converse with God, show Him you love Him, and show him you are willing to place him first in life. Start easy by getting up in the morning and just saying, "Thank you God for this day." Move into prayer at mealtimes. Pray at every meal, together as a family. Slowly, you will find that you can do this easily every day. Daily devotionals are available online, through cell phone applications and even the old-fashioned way - through books. Use them! Once you start placing God first in your life through prayer, the rest will fall into place. Praising and praying to God can help you overcome tremendous obstacles in your life.

Have you ever felt as if life were just passing you by as you sit on the curb? This happens to me, especially when I am struggling with where God needs me, and I feel like everyone else is just enjoying the ride, while I sit in sorrow. I know when I get into this pit that God will guide me out, but I just cannot find the ladder to climb out to Him. After TJ, our second child, was born, my life seemed so complete. Megan was one and a half years old and running around the house while I tended to TJ. Even during this time of joy, I found myself in the midst of depression and sitting on the couch most of the day. While I never recognized that I was digging my pit deeper and deeper, my friends did. My dear friend, Carol, called me one day and encouraged me to join a women's group. This group was a beautiful witness to the community. Their mission was to donate to the community with their time, talents and dollars. Carol had been part of this group for over a decade and enjoyed her time with the women tremendously. She could see I needed something in my life. Just by her mere suggestion, my life took a turn. I found that the gifts that God gave me could be used to help others, and that is all I needed. Carol was my angel during that sad time, and I cannot thank her enough for guiding me gently out of that pit and up that ladder of hope.

We need God desperately in our lives, and sometimes it just takes someone special to help us find Him. Moses recognized this in the battle of Amalek. Moses told Joshua to engage in the battle with Amalek. Standing at the top of the hill with Aaron and Hur, Moses would hold the staff of God in his hand. As Moses raised his arms, the Israelites battled fiercely; as Moses' arms fell, the battle would fall to Amalek. As you can imagine, Moses' arms grew weary, so Aaron and Hur supported his arms on either side.

I could use that kind of support in my prayer life. Sometimes I just grow weary and tired of prayer. Usually God will use my family to support me when this happens. My 13 year old daughter, Megan, will inspire me to go to the Adoration Chapel at our church, or my 11 year old son, TJ, will read me an excerpt from his saint book. They remind me of the importance God holds in our lives. Moses knew it was important to keep God present that day of battle. He knew God was the only reason they would win against Amalek. When planning and preparing for war, it drains the very life out of a person. I am sure Moses was

exhausted physically and mentally. It took his friends and family to support him, and sometimes that is what God is asking us to do. Let go of your pride. You cannot do this alone. Actually, you aren't even supposed to try to do it alone. You must have God.

As your communication with God becomes more consistent, you may find that God will confront you with one of His plans. It can be difficult when God sees strengths in you, which you cannot see. God knows that He can accomplish anything through us if we are open to letting Him work. David and Goliath is a powerful story of obstacles that are too large for anyone without God in his life. Here is David faced with Goliath. David knew God would give him the strength to conquer. He begged for the chance to fight off this giant enemy. By placing God in the highest esteem, David put God first. So many times I have allowed those "giants" in my life to stop me in my tracks. Not only do I sit hunched over, hiding my face from God, so he doesn't choose me for those dangerous battles, but I also run and hide if I can get away with it. Don't choose me. I am not the one you are looking for. Maybe if I avoid eye contact, God won't see me… I seem to back away because I know that I am not strong enough. I forget to decrease me and increase God. As we found out in the story of David, that kind of attitude will not help us to win the difficult battles. God must be first.

Those times when we struggle in life are usually when we have placed ourselves on the front burner and God in the rear (or according to my life – not even on the stove)! David did this later in life when he became king. Power can be a terrible "giant" in life if we allow ourselves to think that WE got ourselves there. David found this out the hard way. By increasing his own strength and decreasing God, David decided it was okay to steal someone else's wife. Bathsheba was a huge temptation to David. Usually when pleasuring our own self, we find that we leave God out of the equation – David sure did. David would soon find out that sinful behavior comes with a price – a hefty one at that. His choices worsened when he decided to have Uriah the Hittite (Bathsheba's husband) killed during battle. David purposely told his soldiers to leave Uriah unguarded so that he would be placed in harm's way. You see Bathsheba was pregnant with David's child. Desperate times often call for desperate measures. God would have no part of this in David's life, so he took David's son. Using the death of David's own son, God showed David once again that He was in control, not David. It opened David's eyes to what he had done and sent him to prayer. After spending time with God, David saw that he once again needed to place God first. Did you realize that David only saw this when he took the time to converse with God? Prayer is the key.

I have been in David's shoes. When the going got too tough for me, I really began praying. Realizing that I took the wheel and pushed God into the backseat, I prayed for forgiveness from God. I just moved right ahead with my own power, pleasure and will, forgetting about what God really wanted and doing what pleased only me. Pleasure is dangerous when we don't involve God in that joy. I have found that when pleasure comes quickly, it is usually because it is my own and I have not considered God's joy into it.

Placing God first seems a bit easier when I am surrounded by family and friends. It's easy when we are dealing with our God centered friendships – don't you think? God called us to be loving neighbors to all, but just what does He mean by that? The parable of the Good Samaritan in Luke is a perfect example of putting God first in your life and doing His will. As you know, the man in the story was a victim of robbery. He had been beaten and robbed, and he was left to die on the side of the road. Both a priest and a Levite walk by and leave the man lying in the ditch. I can't help but think that maybe they were too busy to stop or maybe they were going to get help from someone else, but that is not the story that Jesus chooses to tell this crowd. He says that the only one that would stop was the Samaritan. The Samaritan not only stops, but he aids the beaten man, takes him to an Inn, tends to him there, leaves money for the innkeeper to care for him, and then returns to check up on him. Wow! That is extraordinary; especially when you consider that the Samaritan people were the lowest of the low. This story must have surely astounded people who were listening. A Samaritan – really??? There must be a reason that this story was told – Jesus had his reasons for parables that he chose. The priest and the Levite were highly esteemed individuals; people who were thought of as "Godly Men." Do you think that Jesus was trying to tell us that anyone can take God out of the equation, and we are all sinners who need a little dose of humility every once in a while? The priest and the Levite chose to not stop – we don't know why – we just know they didn't stop.

Stopping does not happen often in my life; in fact, my life is centered on busyness. Just today I have a long "to do" list. If I dare to look at my weekly calendar, I might go into overload. Every kid has a doctor appointment this week (on different days, of course), we have repair men in and out, I have a lot of work to get done in the office, I have meetings every night this week at church, and

I haven't even been to the sporting events that I need to attend. Crazy right? Sound familiar? Take a step back. What actually needs to be done? The first thing I did was call into work this morning and ask them to make a list of the projects to be accomplished this week. I am going to go through that and see what I can do from home. I am fortunate that I have a wonderful, supportive husband who from time to time can leave work at 5pm to pick up kids at sporting events. I called and rescheduled a doctor appointment, and I toned down my week. The best part was I opened up time to write more in my book. It allows me to delve into scripture and see my world in a different perspective, which is what I need. By letting go of some of the craziness of life, I have time to refocus on God and let him know I need His help this week. Busyness is one of the most dangerous distracters from God. We can get overwhelmed thinking about all that we need to accomplish, but what can we put aside for much needed time for God? I encourage you to put it aside. Your family will be stronger because of it, and your job will not suffer. God will see to it. Just trust Him.

Here is the best part of the story: the Samaritan was "moved with compassion." This gives me goose bumps because I know this is what God is calling me to do - stop and be moved with compassion. The Samaritan was not thinking of what he had to do that day – he saw it, right there on the side of the road. He felt that dying man's pain. He let go of his busyness and stopped for God. Can you imagine having that much love for someone you don't even know? Can you imagine stopping everything for a stranger in need? God can. He thinks of each of us in that very way. He sees us in that ditch. He picks us up off the side of the road, cares for us, and checks back on us. Don't turn him away; allow Him to help. Don't let your busyness distract you from this great offer from God.

Busyness can be our biggest obstacle in life. I found in my own life that it wasn't always about saying "no" to everything, it was more about saying "yes" to the right things. One question I like to ask myself when I find myself overwhelmed with kids' activities, work, and life in general is this:

"WHAT DOES THIS EVENT HAVE TO DO WITH MY FAMILY'S ETERNAL SALVATION?" This is the toughest and easiest question to answer. It is an oxymoron at its best.

What does Lacrosse have to do with my son's eternal salvation? Nothing.

What does swimming have to do with my daughter's eternal salvation? Nothing.

What does a meeting with the school PTO have to do with my eternal salvation? Nothing.

What does track and cross country have to do with my family's eternal salvation? Nothing.

What does my weekly bible study meeting have to do with my family's eternal salvation? It allows me to place God back in my life and discuss where God is leading me as a mother.

What do my spiritual director meetings every Monday night have to do with my eternal salvation? They encourage me to use my God given gifts to inspire others to become closer to God.

What does my Adoration hour have to do with my eternal salvation? It gives me time in prayer with God and takes me away from my hectic schedule to rest in God's arms.

Can you see what I am saying about why these questions are simple, yet difficult? I know my kids love their sports, music, and all other activities at school. It requires a lot out of me to get them there and back home, but if I am forgoing my time with God for these events, maybe I need to rethink them. If I am giving up prayer time because I am driving to lacrosse practice, maybe I have made the wrong choice. If I am dropping bible study because I am exhausted from driving kids everywhere, maybe I have made the wrong choice. If I am purposely pushing God out of my life to add in the activities that have nothing to do with my family's eternal salvation, then I may be making the wrong choice. I realize this will make many squirm, but really think deeply about your choices. Balance is the key, and the key to balance is God.

A small group of my friends share an Adoration hour at our church. Because there are several of us, I end up going about once every six weeks. Our hour is on Sunday from 1pm to 2pm. I had many reasons why I just could not help during April, May and June, and I will list them here:

- I cantor at church at 11am and 12:30p, so sometimes I am scheduled for both of those times and am not finished until 1:30pm.
- My kids go to Sunday School at different times. One goes at 8am-9am and the other from 11am-12pm.
- During the months of April, May and June, my son plays lacrosse on Sundays, and his games are anywhere between 1pm and 3pm
- I was traveling out of town on three of the Sundays during this time frame

I am sure you can see why it was so complicated for me to get to Adoration during the months of April, May and June. Did I make the right choice? Yes, I probably made the right choice for that particular time and day for those three months, but I didn't end up making the best choice. You see, I could have picked up another hour on a different day, but I didn't. I just backed out of Adoration and never thought about going in during the week, or early in the morning, or even late at night. After all the Adoration Chapel is open 24 hours a day, 7 days a week. So, you can see why this choice is complicated. Placing God first was difficult, and I failed to see the best option, or maybe I ignored the best option.

God wanted me to be "moved with compassion." Instead I was moved with my distractions. I could only see that I was overwhelmed and needed something to be eliminated. Selfishness is what I chose, certainly not compassion. I needed a giant STOP sign planted on my front driveway. I needed God to call out to me and tell me to WAKE UP! I turned God away, and I certainly didn't allow Him to help. I was distracted by life commitments. Failure to see that God would help me out of my over commitments was wrong.

When I realized that I had let God down, I started to meditate on this verse, **JOHN 3:30**, "He must increase, I must decrease." In fact, I have it written on my bathroom mirror so that I wake up to it every morning. I am so thankful that God gives me His wisdom when I actually listen to Him.

PROVERBS 2:1-2 "My son, if you receive my words, and treasure my commands within you, So that you incline your ear to wisdom, and apply your heart to understanding."

Placing God first in your life may be complicated, but just as the words from Proverbs say; He will give you wisdom to decipher His plan. When you leave God out of the equation, life becomes monotonous and unfulfilling. When you place God first you are filled with love, humility and treasure beyond any wealth.

Study
Questions • CHAPTER TWO

01

Review the four scriptures at the beginning of this chapter. Which one speaks the most to you and why?

02

Is prayer a part of your daily life? Think about how you can increase your time with God each day. Set out a plan and stick to it – start easy. Write your plan below and throughout this study each week. Talk about the difficulties you find following through with your plan.

03

When Moses needed help, he turned to Aaron and Hur to help him. Do you have someone who would help you with your prayer life? Who is that?

04

During the battle that went on between David and Goliath, God gave David strength that no one thought was possible. Have you ever done something that no one thought was possible for you to accomplish? Have you ever stepped up to a ministry that you never thought you would have the time to do? Write down how God helped you accomplish the impossible.

05

Has power ever hit you like it did David? Have you ever been in a situation where you feel powerful and untouchable? Has this position in power ever led you to do things that may be hurtful to others? To help you come up with thoughts, think of power struggles in families, between friends, at work, in your volunteer time, and at kids sporting events.

06

Have you ever found yourself to be too busy for God? What is taking you away from spending time with God? How can you change this for one week of your life? Write a plan to reschedule in God for one week.

07

Looking back on your life, do you wish you had done things differently to make more time for God? In what areas do you think you would have changed things to make room for him? Reflect on the saying "Family First." What does that mean for God, if you consider your family before Him? Think about the disciples; do you think they would have considered family first, before leaving everything and trusting in God?

CHAPTER THREE

CALMING THE RAGING STORMS

Lightning bolts scare me. Just the flash of light in the sky on a breezy spring morning can move me into storm mode. Claps of thunder, which comes so soon after the lightning, remind me of just how close that storm is. My son, who is amazingly brilliant, once told me that thunder is the sound of lightning. The closer the lightning is the sooner we will hear the thunder afterward. This theory was proven to us when we were fortunate to be vacationing on New Smyrna Beach during the very last space shuttle lift off. We watched from the balcony of our oceanfront condo as the final space shuttle mission launched into the sky that bright sunny day. It was amazing. Fifteen minutes after watching this incredible launch, the sound of the shuttle roared down our beach and shook our windows. Wow!! Sound does travel – and we heard it even though the space shuttle was out of sight.

That reminds me of how God works in our lives. The lightning bolt comes first and then BOOM the thunder rolls, and at the end of the storm we will see the rainbow of God's miracle at work. The storm moves in slowly, sometimes with no warning. That first sign of trouble may be the lightning in the distance. We don't hear the sound at first, but we feel and see the lightning strike clearly. The mood of the weather changes, and we can almost smell the rain in the air. That storm is coming, and how are we going to respond to it? The lightning hits like a flash allowing me to see clearly what God wants, and then I need to make a move on that lightning, or do I try to control things myself?

Do I wait it out to see if He really means me, or do I open my heart and listen to the Holy Spirit? When I finally make the move, I hear God's thunder of confirmation, which sets me aback for a minute, because I am fearful of following through with His will. Would he really want this to be difficult for me? He may, since it is all part of the plan. The thunder may last only minutes, but it may last for what feels like hours. Weathering the storm is all part of God's plan. Keeping my eyes open, God shows me a beautiful rainbow when I finally allow the thunderstorms of my life to clear. That rainbow will show me the beauty of allowing God to be first in my life. Sound complicated? It is. Placing God first can be difficult. Storms are scary and disruptive to our lives. Placing God first can be that way too. It is a different way than we are used to. Complete trust in someone else can prove to be challenging. Trust that the storm will pass and that it is okay to struggle a little. Struggling makes us stronger. It also makes us rely on God sometimes for the very first time.

Take Saul (someday would be Paul) for an example. Saul was "breathing murderous threats against the disciples" **(ACTS 9:1-27)**. He was a horrible, scary guy. He went to Damascus to bring back all the followers of Jesus that he could find.

On his way a "light from the sky suddenly flashed around him." *Lightning strike has hit.*

Saul then falls to the ground and hears a voice. "Saul, Saul, why are you persecuting me?" *A little thunder here.*

Saul replies, "Who are you, sir?"

The reply came, "I am Jesus, whom you are persecuting. Now get up and go into the city and you will be told what you must do." Here is where the choice happens. Should Saul follow the words he just heard, or run for the hills?

Saul gets up and cannot see a thing. The Light has blinded him. He goes to Damascus and does not eat or drink anything for three days. *At this point, I think one could assume the storm is raging within Saul.*

In the meantime, Ananias, a follower of Christ, has been called by the Lord to put his hands on Saul and bring the Holy Spirit upon him. Ananias is fearful of this, and rightfully so, since Saul is one scary guy. Everyone had heard of Saul's murderous plan to take all followers of Christ back to Jerusalem and have them killed. Ananias trusted in the Lord and knew that God would be with him and needed him for this dangerous mission. So Ananias went and placed his hands on Saul. "Immediately things like scales fell from his eyes and he regained his sight. He got up and was baptized, and when he had eaten, he recovered his strength." *And the beauty of the rainbow has shown itself clearly.*

Saul turned against all he believed to follow the Lord. He had to leave behind his friendships, his livelihood, and his very reason of existence all for the Lord. All God is really asking is to place Him first. Saul gave up everything to do this. I have tried to do this each day in one little way – let's just say it has been a storm in me trying to implement it.

Maybe today I will ask God before I do anything, kind of like a child asking his mother, "Hey, God, can I take the car out; or Hey, God can I have a snack, or even better, Hey, God can I go have coffee with my friend?"

Have you ever thought of just asking God for a little reassurance that you are making the right choice?

As parents, we may say, "Sure you can go over to Ashley's house, but can you make your bed first?" God may say, "Sure you can go have coffee with Jenny, but would you spend some time with me in prayer first?"

What a concept that would be! Try it for one day and see how it goes. It is not easy, but it is worth every penny.

Moses was a great example of communication with God. Of course, Moses was more a tale of "coerced communication." You see, Moses fled Egypt because he had killed an Egyptian who was beating a Hebrew (one of Moses' people). He knew the ramifications for killing an Egyptian so he fled to Midian. Midian was Moses' escape from the "real world." He thought he could hide, but God found him. God said to Moses that He needed him to lead God's people out of Egypt. The Egyptians oppressed God's people, and God needed Moses to take the lead. What do you think Moses' reply was? I can tell you it wasn't a resounding "yes." Moses debated that he really wasn't the right person for all this. Surely, God must be looking for someone else for this mission. After talking a little self-esteem into Moses, God gave Moses some "tricks" to use on the Egyptians. Hence, Moses feebly confirmed that he would do it as long as his brother, Aaron, could go with him.

When I say having a conversation with God is difficult, imagine what it was like for Moses? Moses did not want to hear God's plan. In fact, he tried to persuade God to find someone new. That is truly what prayer is all about. Persistent prayer is not about praying the same thing over and over (although sometimes that is what happens). It doesn't mean that praying again and again will change God's mind. Persistent prayer is changing our mind to fit God's plan. We

converse with Him. He gives us a little jolt of self-esteem, and we tell Him He is way off base. Then He tells us some tricks to use to get the job done. However, we say, "Well, as long as I can take support with me, then maybe I can handle it." We agree because God shows us He will help us with the plan or at least send some help for us. The important part is God doesn't change, we do, and we change through prayer.

I THESSALONIANS 5:17 "pray without ceasing"

Moses certainly gave me insight into seeing God's will more clearly. It definitely wasn't smooth sailing for Moses. He would encounter many stops, but God would be there to help him weather the storm. Storms make us refocus on what is important. Maybe it is the lack of control we have over them or the sudden realization that we truly are fearful of struggle. There is no doubt in my mind that Moses was scared - scared that the Egyptians would kill him for murdering one of their own. Moses was thrown into a sea of anxiety when he realized what God needed him to do. God had some fierce storms ahead for Moses.

Matthew recounts a story of a storm at sea in **MATTHEW 8:23-27**. The disciples follow Jesus onto a boat that day and suddenly a violent storm wakes them up. Jesus appears to still be sleeping during this tumultuous storm. They of course awaken Jesus. "We are perishing!" Jesus replies, "Why are you terrified, O you of little faith?" Jesus then gets up out of bed and "rebukes" the winds. A great calm comes over the sea and the boat.

According to Matthew's depiction of this situation, the disciples were very afraid and woke up Jesus because they knew he was the only one who could save them. I can't help but think that maybe Jesus wanted them to place God first at that very moment. It never says that the disciples prayed and discerned about what to do. It never says that they actually pleaded for God to help them see a way out of this storm. Maybe instead of waking up Jesus, God wanted them to see that He was there for them. Jesus was soon to leave them. God knew the tortured future that Jesus had ahead. Maybe God wanted the disciples to realize that He was giving them that very same power to calm the storms of all those who believe.

I have to say, if I had been in this situation, I would have been upfront in waking Jesus. "Get him up; he will know what to do. Jesus can help us! We are going to die!" Oh yeah, I would definitely have pushed prayer to the wayside and moved right ahead to the easy road. Why waste time in prayer – we have immediate needs right now! Well, guess what? God doesn't want me to do that. He wants me to really think through a situation and pray for His help and guidance even when time is running out; especially when time is running out. Jesus was going to leave these disciples in order for us to have eternal life. God was ready to give the disciples the strength to yield miracles, to bring healing, and to love unconditionally.

"If I fly with the wings of dawn and alight beyond the sea, even there your hand will guide me, your right hand hold me fast." **PSALM 139:9-10.**

No matter where we are, God will join us. God has given us the strength to see through a day, to take on many different storms.

While reading the book, *Quiet Strength* by Tony Dungy, I came across a chapter that was an instant reminder of the need to place God first in my life. Tony talks about struggling after he was not drafted into the NFL. He prayed that God would give him a "clear sign" on what path to take in life. "…Maybe something plastered on a billboard on the side of the road or flashed on a scoreboard at a stadium or written clearly in the clouds with a divine finger." This wouldn't be the last struggle that Tony would endure during his life. In fact, the amazing part of his book is that his faith helps him withstand life. It wasn't playing football or coaching. It was God. Tony was fortunate to recognize that clearly. Not all of us catch on so quickly – as I have said God tends to use lightning strikes before I notice. Tony refers to the "quiet whisper" that God used for Elijah. That would have never worked for me, but it does for Tony. Tony's storms were violent, but he saw them as easy to calm because God was in the front, blocking Tony's way down to the end zone. You know what the best part is? Tony gives God the credit. He was just following God's will.

Following God will generate many chances for storms. Lightning strikes, thunder rolls and the storm will rise. Just expect it to happen, but more importantly, remember that God will show you the light at the end. He will provide you with a miracle –a rainbow. When you place God first, don't presume life will be smooth sailing, because rough waters may be ahead, but God will give you the tools to conquer. And maybe, just maybe, He is giving you a gift by allowing you to weather that storm. Don't turn it away – jump right in and surf the waves!

Study
Questions •CHAPTER THREE

01

Do you ever move into "Storm Mode" during your struggles? Think of a time
that you really struggled with God's plan for you (death of a parent or child,
child going to college, a change at your place of work, other people who hurt or
irritate a plan of action you have in place). Now think about how you handled it.
What was the initial lightning strike? Then when did the thunder roll in?
Was it a long storm? At what point did you get a glimpse of the rainbow?

02

At any point during your struggle did you actually spend time with God?
Was it a one- time plea for help, was it a constant nagging, or was it more
of a conversation?

03

Moses conversed with God quite often. Surprisingly, Moses doubted his ability
to fulfill God's plan on a regular basis. Has God ever spoken to you or placed
something on your heart that you just didn't think you were capable of doing?
When you decided to take a leap of faith and do it, what changed your mind?

04

I THESSALONIANS 5:17 says to "pray without ceasing." What does that mean to you?

05

MATTHEW 8:23-27 recounts the story of a storm at sea. What would you have done if you were the disciples in the midst of a storm with your savior sleeping on the boat? What does that say about your closeness with God?

06

Read **PSALM 139**. What does this Psalm say about the way God thinks of you? When you call out for help from Him, how does he answer? Are you ever too far away for Him to hear your cry?

07

In Tony Dungy's book *Quiet Strength* he talks about wanting a clear sign from God. How does God usually nudge you to follow His will? (This could be when God called you to be a parent, when God called you to go back to work, when God called you to make tough decisions, when God called you to move, or even when God called you to forgive someone).

08

Do you allow God to calm your raging storms or do you calm them yourself? How can you begin to let God take over the storms in your life?

CHAPTER FOUR

FINDING YOUR HUMBLE SPIRIT

Remember those four concepts (in order to place God first) that were introduced at the beginning of this book from the *Imitation of Christ*?

1. Christ's teaching surpasses that of all
2. Have humility, know your limitations
3. Don't put your trust in riches
4. Center your love on what is unseen not seen

CHRIST'S TEACHING SURPASSES ALL

One of the basic components of Christianity is that you follow Jesus Christ. That is the simplistic view of Christianity, but it is the truth. The first strategy of hearing God's call is to recognize that Christ 's teaching surpasses that of all. While it seems like a relatively easy concept, it isn't. Acceptance and Action are required in this first step. There are many that mentally believe that Christ is King, but there are few who act like Christ is King. As I am sitting in church hearing the readings from the bible, I recognize that I am a sinner and I must do better to live up to Christ's example. Minutes later, I walk out that door and start that bad behavior all over again. Imagine God's frustration. It is a good thing He is patient.

Recently, my family took a trip to Myrtle Beach, SC where my daughter, Megan, competed in a National Junior Olympic Cross Country Race. Watching Megan over the past cross-country season has been awe-inspiring. She started the season with no knowledge whatsoever of what was expected of her. She listened to all her coach had to tell her about the sport and soaked up every word. Not only did she listen, but also she acted on that wisdom and challenge from her coach. It wasn't easy; in fact, it was hard work. She struggled at the beginning. Her asthma flared and her body fought back fiercely. Her perseverance was amazing. She continued the battle taking in the knowledge and acting on it even through the pain. Finally, she found a great balance. Her body gave up the fight, and instead started responding to her hard work. All of a sudden, Megan was quite the runner. Her race times continued to get better, and her attitude remained strong. She knew her body would accomplish just about anything she set her mind to. Because of her team's determination, they qualified for the national competition. I was a proud mama. Just watching her reminded me that God wants me to do the same. He wants me to listen to Him and then act upon it. It won't be easy. It may make me squirm, and I might feel a little pain, but in the end, I will finish the race. Maybe not first, but I will finish with God pushing me forward along the way.

Hearing God and acting on that Word are two very demanding verbs. The definition of the word hear has two parts. The first part means to perceive something by ear, but the second part involves listening with attention. There are many times I have perceived something but not actually paid attention. I am gifted at looking like I am paying attention to my kids when they are talking, but if it is a subject that doesn't engage me; I can tune it out with no problem. Do you think if I do this with my kids, I can do this with God? Absolutely. Usually, when God is talking and I am not engaged, the signs come back to haunt me. I know what God said was important, but I just didn't want to hear it. My stomach will turn upside down, sometimes I will get a headache, or sometimes I will just get stuck in a bad mood. Whatever the sign is, it usually means I am not paying attention to what God is trying to tell me. In fact, I am most of the time doing exactly the opposite of His request.

In our three short years in Utah, Pete and I found ourselves smack in the middle of a building project for our church. The church had been meeting in a small fraternity house on the edge of a university campus. For almost ten plus years, the Parish had tried to raise the funds to build a new structure and had failed to receive the funding from members. The priest struggled with providing all the needed services in the small building, so ultimately he decided to build without the funds. As I am sure many of you know, when financial difficulties come into the picture, life tends to go downhill. The priest was hopeful that God would see this through and eventually provide the funds that were needed. Maybe once the people started to use the new building, the funds would come. During this time, there would be lots of hurt feelings and power struggles among parishioners. Eventually, the new building was constructed but not without a trail of destruction in its path. God probably was trying to tell all of us something in this time, but I don't think any of us were listening with attention. I know personally during that time, I was not placing God first in my life, and I certainly was not listening to Him. I thought I was. I tried to put him first, but my pride got in the way. Humility has been a wonderful realization for me. God showed it to me in a very strong manner, but I needed that. I got a good dose of humble pie, and later I found a way to use that asset in my church today. Not to say pride doesn't sneak up on me once in a while, it does, but I recognize it way more often these days.

In order to truly hear God's teaching (which surpasses everything else in this world), we must pay attention. We must not only accept His teaching, but we must show we accept it, by acting on that Word.

HAVE HUMILITY AND KNOW YOUR LIMITATIONS

Ever heard of "blind ambition"? Max Lucado in his book *God Came Near* has a wonderful reflection on blind ambition. Blind ambition involves tremendous pride, selfishness and determination. Max Lucado calls this "Success at all costs. Becoming a legend in one's own mind. Climbing the ladder to the top. King of the mountain. Top of the heap. I did it my way." Interesting isn't it? Corporate America does seem to thrive on these ideals. Think about this – where is God in all this? The depressing part of all this is – this does not just happen in corporate America. It happens in School PTO's, bible study groups, church committees, little league organizations, and city, state and federal government. I don't know if I can think of an area that this notion doesn't exist. We have all collectively come to believe that success is the key to happiness. Who says? Mother Teresa is quoted as saying, "God doesn't require us to succeed; he only requires that you try."

Hmm. I guess a little dose of humble pie may be what all of us need. I spoke about this earlier. God gave me that bad tasting dish, and I finally snapped out of my feelings of pride. It took me several years before I truly saw what He wanted from me, and even then, I thought, "Are you kidding me? God, are you setting me up to fail?" Yep. That is exactly what He was doing. He wanted me to put all my time and effort into something that I was sure to flunk. He also wanted me to do this in front of the parishioners at our 10,000-member parish. Wow. Really?

Take in this scene. After leaving my very small church in Utah, I came to Indiana where we joined the largest Parish in the diocese of Lafayette. I immediately registered at the church and found great opportunities like bible studies, weekend retreats, choir, stewardship council, and much more. I am not kidding. I dove in like crazy. What I found was that everyone was so professional. I felt a little inadequate. The wisdom that some of the people held in their heart was overwhelming and intriguing all at the same time. After attending a weekend retreat with eighteen other women, I found that God really needed me to step it up. After being in the Catholic Church for eight years, I still did not really understand the Liturgy. I tried, but I just had not quite connected with the beauty and wisdom of the entire Liturgy of the Mass. So I took a big gulp and headed to see our Music and Liturgy Director. Swallowing my pride, I asked him if I would be able to help with the cantoring on Sunday mornings. Cantoring in the Catholic Church involves leading the congregation in song. The cantor's at our church are professional. Sometimes I feel that the level of ability is beyond that of any stage production that I have ever seen. While it makes me wiggle in my seat comparing the cantors to a stage performer, it is truly what I felt during the Mass. They were amazing, wonderful singers. The beauty of their songs of praise radiated from their very soul. Why on earth would God want me to do that? I can hold a tune, but really why not just be in the choir? Nope! I knew the nudge quite well. And it was as if God were pushing me all the way down the hall and through that music room's door. The cantor's vast responsibilities include knowing and understanding the liturgy. My first Mass was unexplainable. I was shaking so intensely that my knees were banging under my choir robe. Where do I sit? How long will it take me to get up and down to that cantor stand? What words should I be listening for the priest to say? What if I make a mistake? What if people know I make a mistake? Why does God want me to humble myself this way? At this point, my good friend, Jeanne, came up to me and said "Just pray. Take deep breaths and breathe in the Holy Spirit and breathe out your pride." She was right. It worked. Did I make a mistake? Yep. I do every week, and each time it happens I smile up at God and thank him for His gift of humility. If I can humble myself in front of an entire Parish, then I can humble myself anywhere. It allows me to place my trust in God, and let Him take over for that hour-long service. After all, it is His song they are hearing, not mine. He is just using my voice to send out His message.

Reminding our self that we really are nothing without God is an important part of placing God first. It certainly can be difficult, and it is against everything we have ever learned, but it is the only way to completely hear God talking to us.

DON'T PUT YOUR TRUST IN RICHES

PSALM 52:6-8 " The righteous will see and fear, and will laugh at him, saying, behold, the man who would not make God his refuge, But trusted in the abundance of his riches, and was strong in his evil desire."

LUKE 16:11 "Therefore if you have not been faithful in the use of unrighteous wealth, who will entrust the true riches to you?"

I TIMOTHY 6:17 "Instruct those who are rich in this present world not to be conceited or to fix their hope on the uncertainty of riches, but on God, who richly supplies us with all things to enjoy."

The desire for wealth keeps our eyes on money and takes our eyes off God. Obviously, this is an opinion, but for the most part, it is true. Wealth can be anyone's downfall. Pete and I have struggled with this for many years. Money can be so incredibly fun, yet it can make people miserable at the same time. Wealthy people exist all around us in our suburban community, since we reside in one of the wealthiest counties in our entire state. The city houses quite a few corporate CEO's, professional sports figures, and many extraordinarily intelligent individuals who choose to live seventeen miles from a large Midwestern city. I grew up in this community, and it provided a tight knit family atmosphere. We all knew each other – or at least knew of each other. Lives were church centered and the community then housed about 10,000 people. Now the city is well over 80,000 people. It has beautiful buildings and concert halls. It definitely caters to the rich. There are still a few of the old neighborhoods that have remained untouched, and their charm is still residing within the people that live there. What has wealth done to the city? It has torn the community apart. Friends bumped heads and parted ways. Constant bickering and disputing exists on the city council. People are fighting over how to spend money, and the love of the community is losing its luster. There are still those few people who really just love the city, not for its wealthy lifestyle or beautiful architecture, but for the people that reside within the city limits. They are still here; you just have to dig past the money to get to them. Those people, who truly portray the beauty of Midwestern America, are the ones who inspire me and show me there is good among wealth.

God calls us to shine out over the money. Let your light shine regardless of what you are worth. When people see you, they don't say "Oh that is the CEO of that big conglomerate." Instead they say, "That man is the most dedicated man to his community that I know. His ability to see good in all and truly love people as a neighbor is amazing." God's light can outshine any wealth, and that is what we should seek.

MATTHEW 5:14-16 "You are the light of the world. A city set on a hill cannot be hidden; nor does anyone light a lamp and put it under a basket, but on the lamp stand, and it gives light to all who are in the house. Let your light shine before men in such a way that they may see your good works, and glorify your Father who is in heaven.

I once heard a funny joke about holding on to possessions, and I wanted to share it with you.

There once was a rich man who was near death. He was very grieved because he had worked so hard for his money, and he wanted to take it with him to heaven. So he began to pray that he might be able to take some of his wealth with him.

An angel hears his plea and appears to him. "Sorry, but you can't take your wealth with you."

The man implores the angel to speak to God to see if He might bend the rules.

The man continues to pray that his wealth could follow him.

The angel reappears and informs the man that God has decided to allow him to take one suitcase with him. Overjoyed, the man gathers his largest suitcase and fills it with pure gold bars and places it beside his bed.

Soon afterward the man dies and shows up at the Gates of Heaven to greet St. Peter.

Seeing the suitcase St. Peter says, "Hold on, you can't bring that in here!"
But, the man explains to St. Peter that he has permission and asks him to verify his story with the Lord. Sure enough, St. Peter checks and comes back saying,

"You're right. You are allowed one carry-on bag, but I'm supposed to check its contents before letting it through."

St. Peter opens the suitcase to inspect the worldly items that the man found too precious to leave behind and exclaims,

"You brought pavement?!!!"

Wealth in heaven is not the same as wealth on earth. That is obvious from the joke. We spend all our days ignoring God so we can be successful, but yet we learn that none of that matters to Him in heaven. So why do we keep doing it? Pride. We need to feel proud of ourselves. We need to feel the challenge of being the best. We need to keep up with our neighbors and look like we are just as good as they are. I know exactly what you are thinking as you are reading this. I can hear you now. I need to send my kids to college. I need to retire in comfort. I need to plan for the future. God wants us to plan for the future, right? Not really. We want to do those things, and they are all great ideals, but God doesn't want any of that – we do. I know I do. We have been saving for years for the kids' college educations and our retirement. We have been planning forever for our future. When it comes down to it, God really doesn't care about that. He just wants us to spend time with Him, so that we can hear His call. That is the joy He wants for us. If you focus too much on the planning and the money, you have taken your eyes off God. This is where Pete and I struggle. How do we carry through with all these plans and still keep God in focus? Planning isn't a bad thing, but keep it in check. Are you taking into account what God is calling your children to be or do with their lives? Have you taken into account what God wants you to do in retirement? Have you taken into account the real reason you are making these "plans"? Pray, read scripture, think deeply about these questions. Are you truly putting the wealth aside and placing God before it? I can already tell you, I am not. I need to refocus my own life. Doing this jolts me back to my daughter Megan and her struggles with running. Remember that pain that I mentioned earlier that my daughter felt as she was progressing in her cross-country training? That is nothing compared to the pain and struggles you will have with this, especially if you are truly blessed with an abundance of money.

CENTER YOUR LOVE ON WHAT IS UNSEEN, NOT SEEN

DEUTERONOMY 6:5 "You shall love the LORD your God with all your heart and with all your soul and with all your might."

I love my kids. I love Italian food. I love Italy for that matter. I love Disney World (any of my family would vouch for that). I love to watch reality television. I love a lot of things. Mostly you could categorize these things to be "seen" items. I can touch, smell, taste, hear, and see all of my favorite items. Loving seems pretty darn easy when you think of it in this manner. It is instant gratification. I eat the pizza, and I taste the love. Ahh, my stomach is full. I watch television, and I can feel my body relaxing from the anxieties of the day. Once again, I have used the "seen" to fill my soul; or so I think fill my soul. All of these simple loves have done nothing to fill my soul. It is like eating candy for breakfast. Two hours later, my stomach is growling. I didn't truly nourish my body, but I felt gratification without any substance.

God is the substance we need in order to truly understand love. God makes our stomachs stop growling for eternity. Hunger will be eradicated with God. God is the "unseen" love. We cannot touch, smell, taste, hear or see Him, but He nourishes our souls like no other. I have found that truly loving God means I have complete faith, trust and hope in His every Word.

Have you ever felt like it is just easier to do things for yourself than to trust that someone else will follow through with it? This has always been a struggle for me, but recently, I have learned the importance of letting others take the lead. I mentioned that I had gone on a church retreat when we first moved back to the Midwest. This retreat was my own personal Road to Damascus (like Saul) which pushed me to place God first in my life. After helping out with many of these retreats, I felt God's call to help in a new way. Each retreat is followed by six months of spiritual formation for the women that attend the weekend retreat. These women will go on to organize and lead the next retreat. This six month period (which meets once a week for three hours) is led by a "spiritual director." Because it is such a big commitment, there are three of us that maintain this ministry. We switch off every six months because the time away from family is sometimes overwhelming. During these six months, we lead the team through

their spiritual journey with Christ. It is important to accept the women where they are and allow them to grow naturally with God. Interfering in this process, or trying to make women jump ahead of the game, can foil God's plan. Even though I know the process quite well, and I certainly know what works and what doesn't work; I have to let the women learn in a very gentle way. Sometimes God does call me to step in, but most of the time He requires me to just remain quiet. Certainly having twenty-five women try to organize a retreat weekend while encouraging them to grow spiritually will be overload for many. The process can be inspiring, and I feel that God blesses each of the groups of women in many different ways. For once in my life, I have to let others move at their own pace – even if I am not comfortable with it. It makes me squirm and move in my seat, but I know that God is working through them. Sometimes, I can see God's light so clearly in our weekly meetings that it is more frightening than the burning bush was to Moses.

God does this with me. He allows me to move at my own pace, making mistakes along the way, and nudging when I need a little help. Loving and trusting in God, who is unseen to all, is hard work. It requires an active prayer life and a constant reflection on His Word. It also requires us to hold His teachings in the highest esteem. Never falter from God's Word because He is the key to eternal salvation. Keep your pride in check. Most people do not recognize pride in themselves; I urge you to look for it. I guarantee you it exists in every one of us; it just presents itself in very different ways. After recognizing your pride, put your wealth aside. Wealth can appear in many varieties. It can be the obvious, which would be money itself, or it can be just the love of money (even if you don't have any), or even coveting your neighbor and all they have. Take it out of the equation and place God over that wealth, so that you can begin to center less on what is "seen" and more on what is "unseen." These four virtues are what made Jesus our role model. Track them down in your life and persevere in the race for God to be first.

Study Questions

• CHAPTER FOUR

01

Think of a time that you heard the Word of God (at church, at bible study, etc). How easy was it for you to hear the scripture and then forget it about it the minute you walked out the door? How can you stop that from happening over and over again?

02

Can you think of a time that God used someone else to speak His Word to you? Tell us about what happened.

03

Has there been a time when you felt like God was setting you up to fail? Has humility ever been placed upon you as a dish of humble pie? How did you feel when you were face to face with failure? Did you recognize then that you are nothing without God?

04

When have you thrown aside God for the pleasure of money? When have you struggled with spending or saving money? Do you currently give to your church or other organizations like you should? Do you struggle with the concept of tithing?

05

Reflect on **DEUTERONOMY 6:5**. What is the difference in the way you love the "seen" versus the "unseen"? Give examples of the two and compare and contrast the love that you show and the feeling you get from loving these things (long term versus short term benefits; short lived feeling versus a longer feeling of love; the emotions that you feel when you are with the seen versus the unseen).

06

Have you ever felt it is easier to do things for yourself than to let someone else do it for you? How does this relate to your relationship with God? Do you let Him take the reigns or do you?

07

Read **MATTHEW 5:14-16**. Is your light hidden or out for all to see? How do you want people to see your love for God? Would you rather have your spiritual life hidden away in a closet, shining for all to see, or somewhere in between?

08

I TIMOTHY 6:17 says "Instruct those who are rich in this present world not to be conceited or to fix their hope on the uncertainty of riches, but on God, who richly supplies us with all things to enjoy." Do you fix your hope on the riches of God or the riches of this materialistic world? How can you show God that His riches are more important than material wealth?

CHAPTER FIVE

BELONGING TO CHRIST

"Will you let me be your servant? Let me be as Christ to you. Pray that I will have the grace to let you be my servant too." These are beautiful lyrics from "The Servant Song." Truly to place God first in your life requires you to become servant-like. Servant certainly has a very derogatory tone to it, doesn't it? I mean how many of us truly like being someone's servant? It sounds like we are giving up everything and lowering ourselves to be like the lowly. Ouch. That doesn't sound like joy. What happened to the joy that God wanted to share in, right? It's there, but in a different way than you could ever have imagined.

John's account of the notorious feet washing at the Last Supper is in **JOHN 13:12-17**. When he [Jesus] had finished washing their feet, he put on his clothes and returned to his place. "Do you understand what I have done for you?" he asked them. "You call me 'Teacher' and 'Lord' and rightly so, for that is what I am. Now that I, your Lord and Teacher, have washed your feet, you also should wash one another's feet. I have set you an example that you should do as I have done for you. I tell you the truth, no servant is greater than his master, nor is a messenger greater than the one who sent him. Now that you know these things, you will be blessed if you do them.

Jesus places himself as a servant in this scripture. He does the unthinkable. He washes the feet of his disciples. It was not a pedicure in today's age where we take our clean little toes and soak them in a hot bath. No this was truly ugly work. People did not have much for shoes back then. They walked through streets without sewage and drainage systems, no sidewalks, and only dusty dirty paths. People used the outside as bathrooms, and animals roamed freely. Feet were disgusting by the end of a day. I am going to go out on a limb here and suggest that showers weren't happening either. So for Jesus to bend to the floor and wash the disciples' feet; he was truly serving in the lowest form. He looked past their dirt and soiled feet. He saw the disciples as something much more. They were carrying on Jesus' mission. They were special all the way down to their toes, and He loved them dearly. Can you imagine what it would be like to have Jesus clean the dirt off your feet? The overwhelming amount of love that filled that room must have been inspirational. All the emotions in the room would have been shown on each of the disciples' faces. Can you imagine what they must have all been saying, "No Jesus, you cannot wash our feet. We should wash yours." Tears of amazement must have engulfed that room. Doubts of their own abilities, knowing that Jesus placed so much trust in them, probably went through their heads. I am sure they felt strengthened just by the trust that He placed within their souls. Jesus looks pasts our dirty and soiled souls too. Beauty is all He sees. He doesn't mind serving us because He loves us so much even through our sin.

Taking this to the next level, we need to find a way to serve others, as Jesus served the disciples. We are all given gifts from God to help us to serve. Using these gifts sometimes requires us to change our lives. According to the *The Servant, A Simple Story of the True Essence of Leadership* by James C Hunter, "Change takes us out of our comfort zone and forces us to do things differently, and that's hard. Challenges to our ideas force us to rethink our position and that's always uncomfortable. Rather than working through things and tolerating hard work and discomfort, many are content to stay forever stuck in their little ruts." Don't fall into this trap. Ask for God's help. He will show you your gifts so that you can serve, just as Jesus did.

Sometimes when we are doing our best (or what we think is our best) to serve God, we find that our burdens become too much to handle. Why on earth would God call us to do this and make it too much? Overload is something that I know personally. I love to say, "Yes." God does give us the wisdom to discern our call. When our lives aren't quite putting God first, and we keep saying that word yes, we aren't truly doing God's work. All of those obstacles that we talked about earlier (lack of humility, love of worldly possessions, not truly hearing God's Word and love of the seen rather than unseen): they can truly block our ability to discern. We think we are doing God's work, but actually we are taking on way too much. We may even be taking a ministry from another person. Overload can cause heavy burdens for us to bear. **MATTHEW 11:28** says, "Come unto me, all ye that labour and are heavy laden, and I will give you rest." This scripture is telling us to rest in the Lord. Resting in the Lord does not mean take a nap. It means allowing God to ease our burdens. We must listen to our true discernment and return to spending time with God and placing Him first. The reward is rest from our afflictions.

Discernment can be difficult when we are not right with God. Once Pete and I moved back home, I took a leap into the political arena. My father had dabbled in small town politics and he personally took quite a hit when he ran for the mayoral office as the incumbent mayor. My personal thought on this was that politics can be dirty business, and I really wanted (maybe even needed) to dive into that world to feel my dad's own pain. I had struggled for years with the personal attacks on my own father, and I needed to put myself in that place to understand why he put himself through that. I can honestly say that during that few months of running a campaign, I found a world that I really did not want to see. Not only is politics cutthroat, but also we can see friends in a whole different light. Power and greed are so common among elected officials that God sometimes does not have a place. Not all circumstances are like this, but from my vantage point, the majority of the political figures definitely struggled with leading by authority and power instead of leading with humility. Reflecting on this time, I can see that God really was not in my plan to run for elected office. It was me, seeking out my own interests, maybe even a little bit of a vendetta. When I came to this understanding, I allowed God to use this mistake for good. I stay active in the governmental process, and I try to stay in touch with what is going on in the big scheme of things, but I know that my calling is not holding political office. Keeping politicians aware of their constituents is more my calling. Fortunately, I was able to place myself in my father's shoes, and I did have some healing for that particular situation. I definitely needed the healing, so I thank God for that gift. Discernment can be tricky. Once again, I go back to the pleasure principle – if it seems to please you quickly and God cannot share in the joy, it is probably not God's will.

Fear is another obstruction of discernment. Fear takes your eyes off God, and it places your eyes on fear. Victoria Osteen, a wife, mother of two children and a co-pastor of Lakewood Church in Houston, TX, wrote a beautiful story of conquering fear. On her website she writes this story:

"There's a story about a woman who was newly divorced, almost penniless, afraid of public places, and trying to raise two teenage sons. After several tragedies in her life, she developed severe agoraphobia and was afraid to even leave her house. She searched her heart for ways to support herself and her two sons.

She loved to cook, and all she knew to do for income was to make sandwiches and other simple foods. With the help of her two sons, she found a few customers; but because she was so uncomfortable leaving the house, she had her two sons deliver the sandwiches. Her business quickly grew beyond the size of her kitchen, and she now faced a decision. Would she stand still and stop growing, or would she confront her fears and step outside her comfort zone? Though fear constantly nagged at her, she recognized that cooking was a desire that God had placed inside of her. As she sat in her house, she could imagine her business growing and began to see success. She made a decision to stretch herself - one step at a time. First, she decided to confront the agoraphobia that imprisoned her. Reaching deep inside herself, she was able to take a job as a chef at a local hotel, and once again she experienced tremendous success.

She was learning step by step that the gifts inside of her were seeds of greatness. A few years later, she opened her own restaurant, The Lady and Sons, right in the heart of Savannah, Georgia. The restaurant's reputation quickly spread, and before long, the restaurant received national recognition.

Paula Dean's restaurant was such a success that she eventually landed her own TV show, published cookbooks, and even had a role on the silver screen. Today she is one of America's most beloved television chefs, and it all started when she realized that the power that dwelt inside of her was greater than the fear that held her back. "

Fear can be conquered, but first we must recognize that fear is holding us back from doing God's will. Until we are ready to define what is holding us back, we will never be able to place God first in our lives.

Let's consider Peter's Denial of Christ and how fear played a role in his decision to deny Christ's existence in his own life.

LUKE 22:54-62.
Having arrested Him, they led Him away and brought Him to the house of the high priest; but Peter was following at a distance. After they had kindled a fire in the middle of the courtyard and had sat down together, Peter was sitting among them. And a servant-girl, seeing him as he sat in the firelight and looking intently at him, said, "This man was with Him too." But he denied it, saying, "Woman, I do not know Him." A little later, another saw him and said, "You are one of them too!" But Peter said, "Man, I am not!" After about an hour had passed, another man began to insist, saying, "Certainly this man also was with Him, for he is a Galilean too." But Peter said, "Man, I do not know what you are talking about." Immediately, while he was still speaking, a rooster crowed. The Lord turned and looked at Peter. And Peter remembered the word of the Lord, how He had told him, "Before a rooster crows today, you will deny Me three times." And he went out and wept bitterly.

Fear stopped Peter from doing God's will. Fear caused Peter to stray from what he knew was right and move toward what was easier. Fear had to be destroyed before Peter could return to Christ and be His apostle. Peter knew what he had done – that is why he "wept bitterly." Once he acknowledged that fear was holding him back, and accepted Christ's forgiveness (which he gave to Peter before this event occurred), then Peter could move forward with God's plan. After all, Peter would become a great faithful servant for Christ, and he would someday be called the "Rock."

A perfect example of servant hood and discernment would be Christ's own mother, Mary. She said yes. Luke writes in **LUKE 1:38** "Let it be done unto me." Her relationship with God was perfect. I cannot even imagine. Never did she doubt in God's flawless plan. She just said yes. She didn't care what others thought of her unwed motherhood. She did question how this all was going to work, but never what others would think of her. If only I trusted so much in God's plan, that I would just say yes. I know what happens when I say yes. There

is change in my life, but sometimes struggling because many times I have to place those great pleasures that I have on the back burner. Mary didn't care. "She was ready to be an unwed mother, a refugee, a widow, and the mother of an innocent man who would be executed as a criminal."

This sounds like humility to me. Maybe, that is the question we should ask ourselves during discernment – where is the humility in all of this?

Mary is a role model for me. Just because I know there may be rough waters ahead, I should take the plunge. Dive right in. She did it, so I can too. When I decided to write this book, I knew the timing was off. Kate had just started a new school; we were just beginning to get hold of her behavioral problems. I have a blossoming thirteen year-old who needs my guidance (even if she doesn't want it), I have an eleven year-old who needs my attention, and I just added hours at work. I wasn't really sure God wanted me to get started right then, but something happened. I was sitting in our Adoration Chapel at church, and I began handwriting my thoughts. The next thing I knew, I was outlining the book and had handwritten Chapter 1 and 2. The next week, I went back to Adoration and read through my words. I was astounded. It didn't even sound like me. It was almost as if God had used my hands to write His words. I knew then, that regardless of whether or not the book is published, I needed to spend time with God writing His words. Maybe it was for my kids, maybe it was for my friends, or better yet maybe it was for me. The time I have spent studying scripture, reflecting in prayer, and rereading great books that inspired me; it all has brought me back to God. It reminded me that all could be accomplished when I just can be His servant. Don't get me wrong! Writing this book was a constant power struggle between God and me. I struggled with what people might think if they read this book I wrote. Would people think I was a hypocrite? Would people think that I was a "high and mighty" follower of Jesus? Would people think I desired fame and fortune from a book, so I chose God as the topic to entice them into my world?

I struggled with this continuously throughout the entire book process. What I realized is that I had opened myself up to God so honestly and so deeply that it was imminent that these doubts pop into my mind. God and I knew the reason for this book was so much deeper than money, fame and fortune. I needed to write this. I needed to get back on track with God. I so desperately needed it, that God was willing to use me to write the words that I needed to hear, and so many others too. We all struggle with our relationship with God. It can become overwhelming when we are not utilizing the gifts God gave us to form a bond with him. That is where I was. I knew there was more to my relationship with God, and I needed to find it once again. Yes, it seemed like overload at times to sit at my computer for hours typing, studying scripture and finding the perfect words for this endeavor. God knew it would be a struggle for me. He knew I needed to be out of my comfort zone. Servant hood does that. It takes us down to the bottom in order for us to receive a glimpse of the top with an entirely new perspective. Looking at God after laboring through this book made me realize, I really had never seen Him from this view. Servant hood gave me just that; without the pride and worldly view that I had become accustomed to.

Study Questions

● **CHAPTER FIVE**

01

What does being a servant mean to you? Does it have a positive or negative meaning?

02

Read **JOHN 13:12-17**. How would you have felt if you were a disciple and Christ bent down to wash your feet? Would you have felt overwhelmed with the responsibility he was entrusting you with? Talk about this story and what it really means to wash another's feet in this world.

03

According to the book, *The Servant, a simple story of the true essence of leadership*, change is difficult. It takes us out of our comfort zone and forces us to do things differently. Does being a servant of Christ make you squirm a little? What is blocking you from doing God's will? List out what commitments are keeping you from Christ.

04

Have you ever experienced overload? Talk about the overwhelming experience that pushed you over the edge. Did you take on too much? Did you ask for God's strength? Do you reevaluate what is important and restructure life so it isn't so overwhelming? Explain.

05

Discernment is a difficult concept. Read the story about Paula Dean in this chapter. What is stopping you from discerning God's call for you? What are your distractors?

06

Mary is a perfect model of discernment. As humans, we are incapable of perfection, but we can find traits of Mary in ourselves. What traits of Mary do you have (humility, unconditional love, fearlessness, don't care what others think, loving mother, open to God's plan, or come up with your own)?

07

Think of a time that you lowered yourself to servant hood, when you actually found yourself at the bottom of the totem pole. How did you react to that? What did it feel like? Looking back, can you see God working through you as His lowly servant?

CHAPTER
SIX

RECOGNIZING EVIL IS FOR REAL

Honesty is the best policy, right? Well, honestly I struggled with this chapter. Once again, I could not take my pride out of this book. I realize that people do not like to talk about the devil. Some people do not even recognize that there is a devil. In my own opinion, I am going to tell you some stories where I know the devil was present. Some are biblically based and some are just personal stories that I have heard. One thing I know for sure is that the devil tends to rare his head when a person is doing something great for God. Evil does not like to see good prevail. The devil will use anyone to stop God's plan from shining through. It doesn't mean that the devil resides in that person; it just means that the person left a crack for evil to seep inside, and for a moment (because that is all he needs) he takes charge. I have been that person that allowed evil to work through me. I have shared stories with you about my struggles with evil working in my life. If evil were left out of this book, then I would have failed in showing the truth of placing God first. It doesn't come without battles, but God will provide us all we need to fight off the attack. We must be on our toes because evil can work through anything and anyone.

GENESIS 2:9 "Out of the ground the LORD God caused to grow every tree that is pleasing to the sight and good for food; the tree of life also in the midst of the garden, and the tree of the knowledge of good and evil."

I SAMUEL 16:14 "Now the Spirit of the LORD departed from Saul, and an evil spirit from the LORD terrorized him."

JEREMIAH 25:32 "Thus says the LORD of hosts, "Behold, evil is going forth From nation to nation, And a great storm is being stirred up From the remotest parts of the earth."

LUKE 6:45 "The good man out of the good treasure of his heart brings forth what is good; and the evil man out of the evil treasure brings forth what is evil; for his mouth speaks from that which fills his heart."

MATTHEW 6:13 "And do not lead us into temptation, but deliver us from evil."

MATTHEW 16:23 "But He turned and said to Peter, 'Get behind Me, Satan! You are a stumbling block to Me; for you are not setting your mind on God's interests, but man's.'"

JOB 1:6 "Now there was a day when the sons of God came to present themselves before the LORD, and Satan also came among them."

The scriptures reference Satan and evil numerous times in the bible. One well-known story of Satan working to do evil is within the book of Job. Job was a wealthy landowner that had ten children and lots of livestock. Satan told God that the only reason that Job was a faithful servant was because he had everything that he needed. God agreed to let Satan test Job to see if his faithfulness continued even through affliction. Satan first took away all of his livestock, ten children and his many servants. Soon after this, Satan resumed his attack by giving Job a horrible skin disease, which resulted in painful boils. After this his friends came and sat with him for seven days before he began to speak. Job was working through these afflictions trying to figure out what he had done to God to make him so mad. His friends were no help. They all manipulated the situation to make it look like Job was at fault for what had happened to him. Their so-called wisdom was irritating Job. God at this point steps in and reminds him that he needs to be brave and conquer this evil working in his life. He offers Job the strength to get through this difficult time of tragedies in his life. Persevering with strength through the trials enables him to become closer to God. Because of his faithfulness, God presents Job with twice the amount of land, more children and a very long life.

As you can see, Satan was not only working through Job, but also through his friends. Without a doubt, his friends thought they were being helpful, but in the end they were allowing the doorway Satan needed to get to Job. This makes me wonder how many times I have done this to my own friends? Instead of allowing them to work through their struggles on their own, I chime in my own ten cents. Is God really calling me to do that? Does he maybe want my friends to see through their own struggles?

Seeking out advice for our struggles is a natural impulse, especially for women. My question is this: have we gone directly to God first before going to our friends? God wants us to go to Him. He wants to strengthen us through our trials. We so desperately need the light to get us through the darkness, yet we keep seeking it in every place but where the light is. The light dwells with God, not our friends. It impresses me that Job stays silent for seven days. It seems he is truly working through the demons in his life to escape the darkness. His friends recognize that he needs time to reflect on what has happened in his life. After all, his whole world has been eliminated. All that he owned and knew to be his was gone. What was missing from his life that he needed to see? This would be difficult for any of us to come to grips with.

ISAIAH 30:19-21 "O people in Zion, inhabitant in Jerusalem, you will weep no longer. He will surely be gracious to you at the sound of your cry; when He hears it, He will answer you. Although the Lord has given you bread of privation and water of oppression, He, your Teacher will no longer hide Himself, but your eyes will behold your Teacher. Your ears will hear a word behind you, "This is the way, walk in it," whenever you turn to the right or to the left."

Looking back, I can see the times that I let evil work through me. Most people would gasp at the thought that evil could work through their souls, but trust me, it does. A friend of mine loves to call me with all the good gossip.

She has great stories of tortured souls who don't seem to ever make the right choices – at least in her eyes. I inevitably get caught up in these tales of woe. My heart sometimes breaks for the person whom my friend is portraying. Dramatic tones and stories cause me to become engrossed in her tale. The next thing I know, I am repeating it to another friend. As the words come out of my mouth, I stutter out the story because I know half of it is untrue. In the past year, I have tried to listen to my friend's tales with a little more caution. I know she needs to talk with someone. I know she is seeking comfort in her own life. When I find myself listening to her demean other's lives, I am now determined to pray for God to let my friend see His Light. Let her see that her path is crooked and going into darkness. Let her see the good in others, not just the evil. You see, when I participate in her conversations, I am helping her spread evil. So, now I try to find the light of God working through her. Trust me, it is not easy. Sometimes I still fall into the trap that she weaves because it is so creatively fascinating. Fortunately, I recognize this now and try my best to understand what God wants me to do for her.

"Help us not to talk too much because talking too much is like driving too fast. Sometimes the brakes are not good, and we pass by the place where we intended to stop. When we talk too much we know we go beyond the truth." **FROM THE BOOK, "GOD IS NO STRANGER"**

I am so fortunate to have a small group of ladies that meet out of our houses for bible study every week. We are from all different faiths and are on very different paths, but we all have the same goal in mind – finding a place for God in our busy lives. Recently we have been studying the book of James. This is a book on friendship, following God's will, and thinking before you speak. During our last meeting we were discussing gossip and what it does to hurt others and ourselves. It enlightened all of us with the strength to really watch what we say. Being aware of what we say to others takes an enormous amount of work. In fact, it takes prayer and thoughtful consideration before even speaking one word from our mouths. Ultimately everything we speak comes from our heart. One of my friends spoke out saying that she always felt even if the words coming out of her mouth were not acceptable to others that God truly knows what is in her heart. She stumbled at the thought that her poor choice of words are from her heart, and yes, God does know that. It was quite a shocker to us all. I cannot help but think of the times my words have caused destruction in others' lives.

When women gather together, there often is a constant fight for positioning. In school PTO's, in church groups, and at work, you will find that women struggle to gain attention and to be liked. Most gossip can be pinpointed back to the fact that we just want people to like us. Pleasing others must be engrained in women. What is left out of the equation when we please others? We are not pleasing God, but we are pleasing others. Evil finds its opening in gossip. When we spend time discussing and degrading others, we are allowing evil to work in our lives. Words that degrade one person are meant to lift another person higher. I talked about this problem earlier – it is called pride. Pride can open up evil within us and to those to whom we are speaking. Just by uttering one negative thought to another, we are placing that thought in the other person's mind. They will harbor our resentment, just like they were the one hurt. We have slandered another person just by speaking something that may be true in only our minds.

My husband is a wonderful servant of Christ. One of his best and worst character traits is he thinks before he speaks. I am not kidding you when I say he thinks before any word comes out of his mouth. Even to the point that when you call our house, if Pete answers the phone, there will be a long pause before he says, "hello." I tease him about this often. And say, "Really, you have to think before you say the word hello." He is on guard all the time with his tongue. Truly, he is an inspiration to me because my tendency is to talk without thinking. Go with my instinct. Lay it on the line. Let everyone know my true feelings. That is my attitude. Pete on the other hand, considers the person, prays about what should be said, examines all angles of a conversation and analyzes the person before speaking. That is what makes him such a great leader. He cares about everyone and wants him or her to hear what he has to say, clearly. My way of communicating allows evil to infiltrate constantly. Pete caulks up the cracks of evil communication with prayer and thoughtful consideration of his words.

Gossip is one of the easiest ways to sin, but another way that comes to mind is liability. Evil can come in the form of blame. As a society, we engrain in our children that taking responsibility for our actions is a bad thing. Blaming others for my own mistakes has been my forte for many years. Impulsively, I don't like to take the blame even if it truly was me. A brightly colored light bulb went off in my head the other day, as I watched and heard my son blame someone else for his own wrongdoing. After leaving the door open to the outside garage, our dog took off to embrace the freedom of the outdoors. That might be okay, if she

would return when I called her, but that is not the case with our dog. My son immediately started to blame his sister and then his friends. He was so determined to blame someone that he started to bring up bad traits that his sister had shown minutes earlier. All of this is going down while our dog runs throughout our neighborhood. My first thought was to yell at him, but in place of this I decided to let him go find the dog, and then I would approach the subject. While the kids were scampering through the neighbors' yards, I had time to think about what had happened. Where had he learned this blame game? Hmm. Let's just say the apple doesn't fall far from the tree. Yep, I had taught him this evil trait. You wouldn't think of this as evil, but it is allowing evil to work through my own sins. I realized that I had to teach him that taking the blame is not shameful. After returning with a very tired dog, my son and I had a talk. I asked him once again to explain to me what had happened. He didn't want to say that he had failed to ensure the door was shut as the little ones came in, and he certainly didn't want to say that he had failed to check to see where the dog was located. Once I explained that I really was looking for him to point out his own liability, not others, he finally relinquished. I assured him that there was nothing wrong with humbling himself and taking the blame. In fact, God rewards us for doing so. Instead of unearthing everyone's faults, I wanted him to concentrate on what he could control – his own fault. After all this, I took it to heart. I too needed to follow my own advice. I needed to admit my own faults and guilt in situations in order to eliminate the devil's work in me.

During one of my weekly meetings at my church where I come across many women who suffer deeply in their relationships with their children, husbands, family members and even God, I have found that I judge people wrongly multiple times a day. The devil seeps into my soul when I judge people in the grocery, at church, at my kids' school, and at home. That sneaky devil slithers into my own heart and uses my judgmental mind to rage a war within my very own body. In my mind, I know that God is the ultimate and only judge of all mankind, but I just cannot help myself. When I see that so-called perfect person at church, I just make assumptions that are not always true. Those assumptions then become the "truth" in my mind, and I use it against the very people I am judging. It sounds awful as I write this on paper. In fact, I cannot believe I allow it to happen, but the truth is – it does.

Living in the very community in which I have spent all my childhood years, makes this even more difficult. Through my own church, I come across people that I grew up with and attended school with. I have preconceived notions about what they are like – I admit it. Usually I cannot shake the feeling I get when I see these people. Sometimes, I find myself hiding to escape having to speak to them. At one of the weekend retreats that I lead as the spiritual director, I found myself face to face with a past acquaintance. Not only was I uncomfortable, but also I was shaking in my boots. You see, I give a personal witness at these retreats in which I speak about very personal situations. God has given me the strength to talk about all these trials that I have experienced, but I also trust that He will bring women to the retreat that need to hear this and will hold my confidence close to their hearts. As I glanced out at this woman, I had my doubts that she would keep my secrets. After all, she certainly wouldn't have kept it years ago. I turned to prayer. God placed on my heart that weekend that I had spent my whole life judging others in my past and not letting go of that heartache. His gentle nudges all weekend made me realize a side to this woman that showed a loving, kind and humble human. Her eagerness to accept God showed me a different side of her. I actually witnessed God's light within her for the first time. By allowing God to work through my own heart, I saw why God loved this woman.

Judging people can be dangerous to our spiritual life. I knew after this weekend, that I had to change my ways. To continue to receive the fullness of Christ's Grace and Mercy, I needed to change. Evil had found a crack in my soul, and I was ready to close that gap completely. When judgment begins in my mind, I ask God to show me where I too fall into sin. I ask God to give me the wisdom to find fault in myself so I can understand the other person more closely. By trying to relate to the person whom I judge, I find a bond with her, and my judgment turns to love and empathy.

ACTS 20:28 "Be on guard for yourselves and for all the flock, among which the Holy Spirit has made you overseers, to shepherd the church of God which He purchased with His own blood."

If we continue to let evil work through us, even in these minor ways, we are letting the devil win. Our eyes will always be on the sin and not on God. Placing God first in your life means you must watch for evil. Be on guard at all times. Never doubt the work of the devil, but most importantly never doubt the strength of God.

Study
Questions

• CHAPTER SIX

01

Reflect on the bible verses at the beginning of the chapter. Do you think evil is for real? Do you believe in the devil?

02

Job proved to be a faithful follower to God even through the trials and tests that Satan placed in his life. Think of a particular time when you faced a very hard time. Talk about this experience. Did Satan win out or God? What can you do for future struggles to make sure that God prevails?

03

Read **ISAIAH 30: 19-21**. What does God promise he will do when you cry out to Him? Why does it say your Teacher will no longer hide Himself? Was he hiding or are the people of Jerusalem keeping him from being seen in their hardened hearts? Do you do this during times of turmoil – fail to see God's Light?

04

When have you let evil work in your life? Consider your sins, and think of how that is a hole to letting the devil seep into your life.

05
Read **MATTHEW 16:23**. Why is Jesus so harsh with Peter?

06
Judas allowed evil to work within his life. Consider the scripture **LUKE 22: 47-53**. What do you think was going on in Judas mind as he kissed Jesus and actually went through with the betrayal? Think about the guilt that he must have felt to actually commit suicide later. What do you think Jesus was thinking at that moment of the kiss knowing his friend had betrayed him and would later commit suicide over the fact.

07
Consider the people that surround you (friends, family, etc). How does the way you handle yourself show the light of God? What about evil?

08
Have you ever found that taking the blame for something is rewarding?
Think of a situation at work, home, or anywhere you choose where something happened, and no one wanted to take the blame. Can you reflect back on that time and find where you could have done something to make the situation better and you chose not to? Or maybe you chose to make it better. Write down your blame here. Do you think there is shame in taking the blame?

09
Do you think letting the devil work in these minor areas of your life truly stops God from being first in your life? How or how not?

10
Make a plan to recognize one sin that really allows the devil to work through you. During the week, try to recognize that sin, and make a plan to ask God for help.

CHAPTER SEVEN

ADMIT IT! YOUR LIFE NEEDS GOD

It's a beautiful day in April. You can smell the grasses pollinating and the blossoms on the crab apple trees. The air is filled with the scent of spring. All you want to do is be outside on the glorious day that you have waited so long for.

The winter has been harsh and cold, and the first occurrence of spring just drives you outdoors. You place everything on hold, just to enjoy some time in the sun. When was the last time you saw or felt the heat of the sun? It seems like months ago. Sitting in the sun, you feel the rays heating up your skin. Your whole body warms and feels rejuvenated. You cannot help but feel happy and peaceful. It is a wonderful feeling. Aren't you glad you gave up some of those errands, just to sit and soak in the sun?

When God is first in your life, this "burst of Spring feeling" is how you will feel every day. God is the heat of the sun, allowing your body to feel joy amidst sorrow and worries. God is this light radiating within your body with strength you thought was hidden away for the winter.

My daughter, Kate, started a new school this past year. At some point during the school day, she was talking with another student about her feelings. The student suggested to her that her brain sometimes does make her feel sad or angry. "This is like storms going on in your head," the student said. The brain can also make you feel happy, "This is like rainbows in your head." What a great analogy. Kate really does struggle with storms in her head, so it gave us an opportunity to figure out how Kate can get from storms to rainbows on her own. One of the great ways that Kate has found to calm her storms is to blow bubbles. There is something about breathing deeply through your diaphragm that allows your body to calm itself. Bubble blowing is a way for a young child to do this. Not only does it allow the body to focus on breathing, but also the outcome is a fun bubble to chase around. The joy comes quickly with Kate when she does this little exercise. It is pretty amazing to watch it unfold.

The question is how do we, as adults, get out of those storms in our lives and back to the rainbows? It isn't easy. First we have to ADMIT we have a problem in our lives. No one is perfect, and God is not asking us to be perfect, but we must conquer the sadness in order to find peace within us. I have outlined steps that follow the ADMIT plan for refocusing on God in your life. You must find a way out of the storms and into the rainbows, before you start to place God first.

- **A**sk yourself, what is truly making me angry or fearful or sad?

- **D**etermine if you can let this situation go, and let God take over.

- **M**ake a plan of action to stop this from happening to you again.

- **I**mitate what Christ would do in this situation, regardless of if it is fair for you personally.

- **T**ake it to prayer daily.

Recently in my life I have had some family turmoil. During this time, I found that my relationship with my sisters and my mother was extremely strained. Without getting into the topic of the struggle, I would like you to see how this ADMIT plan works through my struggle. Let me say that this was a very difficult time for my entire family. We all suffered in different ways because of this one disruption in our lives. Of course it was happening right smack in the middle of the holidays, which just added chaos to the entire problem. My pride and lack of respect for other's feelings made the situation even worse. The amount of pain that I felt was spilling over into my own family also. It was difficult to concentrate on anything but the problem, and my anger was over the top.

ASK YOURSELF – WHAT IS TRULY MAKING ME ANGRY, FEARFUL OR SAD

What is the source of your struggle? Is it you, your family, your work, your church or your friends? I think it was obvious in my case my struggle was between me and my sisters and my mom. I could admit to myself that there was a problem. Now I just needed to figure out what on earth I was going to do to make those rainbows appear in my brain again.

DETERMINE IF YOU CAN LET THIS SITUATION GO, AND LET GOD TAKE OVER.

Pride was definitely blocking my way of allowing God to work in my life. Humility is a constant struggle for me. Like in all arguments, I tend to feel as though I am right and they are wrong. Here is the problem with that win/lose attitude – do you really want to be the "winner" over your family? If the winner and the loser are all part of the same family, then really isn't that just going to cause more turmoil and then doesn't that make you all losers once again? I needed God so desperately to show me what to do, but yet I just could not seem to ask for the help. This part of the process can take time. Both parties in the struggle need to respect that and allow the healing to take place. Letting God take over required that I let go of the problem; not just for a day, but forever. To truly let go, I had to allow myself to heal, so that I could let go forever. I understood my family's side to the story. I knew their feelings were valid and real. I knew they were hurt and distraught by all that was going on. I knew that they needed me to heal quickly so that we could all enjoy Christmas together, but time wasn't working like that for me. It took me several months to finally let God take this over. When I did, that warmth of the sun hit me like a Spring day – it was awesome. I am not going to say that hurt feelings were gone from all parties involved – they weren't, but healing had begun for me.

Being the most difficult step in the process, I highly suggest that you allow yourself lots of time with God during this phase. Actually letting go of a hurtful situation requires you to focus on what is truly important in life. Find quiet, alone time to spend with God. You will need it.

MAKE A PLAN OF ACTION TO STOP THIS FROM HAPPENING TO YOU AGAIN

What caused this struggle in the first place? Try to pinpoint the sin in your life that caused you to get in such a bad spot in your life. Do not allow yourself to blame others at this point. This step requires that you see fault in yourself. It may be how you are handling this struggle or how you perceive what is going on, but you must take blame that you drove yourself into this storm. I definitely took blame in my own prideful attitude. I could spot that a mile away, so could all my family. They knew what was holding me back from forgiveness. Once the healing has begun, a plan of action is needed to stop this from happening again. My plan started with adding God in my life to help me realize that I needed to find humility. I truly needed to find that humility is not such a bad asset. All my life I have been taught that I should stand up for what I believe, don't let others knock me down, keep up the strength to fight the battle, and try to say the hard things that people don't want to hear, but need to hear. Humility was the opposite of that in many ways. Humility requires that I stay silent and pray. Staying away from the limelight and moving toward God is the essence of humility. Reputations and power are non-existent with true humility. It means that I allow God to make the decisions, not me. It means that I learn to hold my tongue when what I have to say does not help a situation. It means that I recognize that the important part of life is to act like Jesus and do what He wants, not what others want. God knows the truth, and that is all that matters. So, my plan was to pray for humility. Let me see the glory in humility; let me feel the peace.

IMITATE WHAT CHRIST WOULD DO IN THIS SITUATION, REGARDLESS OF IF IT IS FAIR FOR YOU PERSONALLY

WWJD. What would Jesus do? I love that movement. What better way to lead your life than to think, "What would Jesus do?" In my struggle, it certainly wasn't hard to see what Jesus would do. He would mend His family. He would let go of His pride and let life go on. He would value all sides of the struggle as valid and real. He would say that you all have a point, so move on. That is what I did. I attended that Christmas party and I moved on. You know what? So did my sisters and my mom. We all moved on. It really wasn't about talking it out. It was my problem to deal with, and my family allowed me the time to deal with it on my own. It was my struggle, not theirs, and they respected that. Once I let that all go, I could see clearly what Jesus would have done.

My father is a wonderful example of this. As I have written in this book, my father had many struggles in the political world. One of the most difficult times was when he ran for office the very last time. After losing the election, my father's opponent chose to continue to gain power by dragging my father's reputation into the dirt. It felt like someone beating our family to the point of no return. He turned my father's life upside down, by making very untrue and unfair accusations after the election. My father stood his ground. He instructed all of us, including himself, not to speak to the media or respond to the accusations in any way. Because he chose to humble himself, the people believed he was guilty. After serving the city for over thirteen years in our beautiful community, my father watched his reputation going down not just in smoke, but in fire and brimstone. I had a hard time understanding why my dad dealt with his struggle in this way, but after spending time writing this book, I see the truth. My dad and God knew the truth. That is all that mattered. Two years after the change of office, my dad's life ended here on earth. I cannot help but see the rainbows in my dad's head as He entered heaven to be with God. His humility through this incredible struggle had ended with peace and eternal life with God. There is nothing better than that!

One of my favorite books, *Having a Mary Spirit* by Joanna Weaver has an entire chapter on Rooting out Bitterness. Joanna Weaver gives the reader three points to consider as we start to forgive others and ourselves:

- Life is unfair
- People will hurt us and let us down
- We won't always understand why

These three points have really encouraged me to place forgiveness in the forefront in order for me to become closer to God. Humility comes to mind as I read her chapter. We have to forgive in order to move on with our life. During this phase – you must learn to forgive. After all what would Christ do?

TAKE IT TO PRAYER DAILY

Most importantly in this ADMIT process you should take it to prayer. Find time to pray every morning, noon and evening with God. Talk over what happened during the day, what your struggles were, and how your "plan" is working. Who knows, God may even help you "tweak" the plan. In my situation, I still struggle with this part of the process. I try to take it to God several times a day, but sometimes the day ends, and through my weariness, I just forget. Once again, God does not call us to be perfect. I do reward myself for acknowledging that I screwed up and forgot to tell God about my day. I do remind myself that I can do better, and then I start the day all over. That is the plan – those rainbows can be found just by waking up and recognizing that this is a new day.

While there are so many biblical examples of placing God first in life, I really want to focus on some everyday people that others or I have encountered. I have a dear friend that I met while in Utah that inspires me still to this day. Her motto in life seems to be "Praise God." She finds the time to thank God each and every day for her struggles, happiness and love of life. Starting her day with a "short" thirteen mile run in the middle of Utah farmland with her headlight on her forehead and her "no slip" booties on her running shoes was Mary's time with God. Whenever I needed anything, I called Mary for advice. Her ability to see the glory of God in all situations is a reminder for me that I need to place God in my life first before all. Mary's life is not an easy one; she has been through many struggles that could have pushed her away from God, but they didn't. She has a wonderful way of presenting God's truth without pushing one to follow her, but you want to follow her. She is magnetic. The energy that surrounds her is vibrant and electric. When I think of where I was with my own prayer life when I met Mary, I cannot believe she continued to lead me. She must have been so frustrated at times by my selfishness, foolishness, and lack of humility. It never stopped her – she continued to evangelize to me. If I had to come up with one word for Mary to define her calling from God it would be – Disciple. She is an inspiration.

Another inspiration is Grandma D, who exudes wisdom from God. My good friend Elizabeth quotes her Grandma D on a regular basis to all of us at bible study. It always starts off with, "Now Darling…" Grandma D had her struggles in life, but she uses those difficult times to find wisdom in all situations.

Elizabeth would bring Grandma D to life for us at our meetings. We would all wait to hear what Grandma had to say about some subject that we were struggling with. Leave it to Grandma to find the right words to ease the situation or the pain. When Grandma was diagnosed with breast cancer, I thought we all were going to cry. Even as she struggles through chemo, Grandma finds good in the pain. Just the other day, Elizabeth and I were jogging and she gave me a Grandma D update. Grandma had gone to get her hair done and seemed to be feeling better after a pretty intense round of chemotherapy. I looked at Elizabeth and said, "Of course she did; who would expect less of Grandma. She is a rock." I wish I could connect with Christ's suffering on the cross, like Grandma D does. I wish I could find the rainbow in all situations. Can you imagine what life would be like if we could all push the storms away?

During a bible study at my church, I became acquainted with two remarkable women. Ellen and her sister Jane are absolutely surrounded by God's light in so many ways. Jane is childlike in her faith. I mean literally childlike. You see Jane has a disability that affects the neurological formation of her brain. Jane's faithful sister, Ellen, is Jane's caretaker. I really have no idea what age Jane actually is, but if I had to take a guess I would say around my age of forty-two. When Jane walks into the room, we can hear her say people's names as she passes by them. One would think that she doesn't recognize us, but she does. If I even walk over to her, she immediately says "Anne Slamkowski, there's Anne Slamkowski." It's an announcement that takes me aback and makes me feel kind of important. "Yeah. That's me. Anne Slamkowski." Each week in bible study, we start off with scripture and song. Jane just belts out the song. She loves to sing God's Word. Hearing her voice just produces a smile on all of our faces. God must be beaming when He listens to her words of praise. During this time, Ellen is just graciously smiling at her sister. The unconditional love that she has for Jane is visible on Ellen's face. Patience, love, and humility are traits that shine through Ellen when she is tending to her sister. While being inspired by her sister, she also feels God's light exuding from her. It must be amazing to wake up each day to Jane, almost like waking up with God every morning. Some people are just placed on this earth to remind us of God's grace - the grace that he offers all of us with no price tag attached. Some of us take this grace as children would, but others stand back wondering: what does God really want for this thing He calls grace? God truly wants nothing, but in my adult mind that is hard to comprehend. I wish I could soak it all in like Jane.

Imagine how many lives you have touched by doing God's will. Now imagine if you actually placed God first even half of the days of your life, the amount of people you would inspire. Each of us has the ability to be a Grandma D, Jane or even a Mary. We all have that potential, if we would just place God first in our lives. Perfection is not the goal. The goal is to do it one day at a time. Each day you will see setbacks, but remember, seeing the mistakes makes you better for the next day. Trust that God will help you, but you must be willing to listen to God's voice on your heart. I guarantee you – your enthusiasm for God will motivate many people to do the same. You may never realize the magnitude of work you do for Him, but you will be happier because you have humbly allowed God to work in your life.

Study Questions

● CHAPTER SEVEN

01

Find a problem or struggle in your life that you are currently dealing with (or in the past) and write it below.

02

Look at the struggle above. What is truly making you mad, sad or fearful in that struggle?

03

Are you willing to let the situation go and allow God to take over?

04

Make a plan to help you stop this from happening again in the future.

05

Think about what Christ would have done if He encountered this struggle. Remember the solution may not seem fair to you. Consider what Jesus would do.

06

The final step is taking it to prayer. Pray daily for strength to follow through with this plan. Ask for God's strength. You have just used the "ADMIT" plan for one struggle in your life.

07

When you are working through a trial, do you feel passionate about there being a winner or a loser? If so, why is that so important to you?

08

Many people think they don't struggle with humility. I believe this is because they don't necessarily know what the definition of humility is. As you have read in my book, humility takes on many different forms of behaviors. Someone who has a competitive mind may struggle with humility. Someone who likes to be in control may struggle with humility. Someone who takes great pride in the works they have accomplished may struggle with humility. Knowing these things, do you struggle with humility? If so, in what ways does that disturb your relation-ship with God?

09

After reading the inspirational stories at the end of this chapter, how can you find more time for God in your life? Do these individuals inspire you to place God first in your life? If those three do not inspire, then who does inspire you? Come up with several traits of those inspirational people that will help you become closer to God?

CHAPTER EIGHT

DO YOU NEED GOD?

Evangelization has always been so frustrating to me. I am not any good at it, and I feel unworthy to tell people that they need God in their lives. I guess it stems from the fact that I know I do not always put God first on my agenda. So, I struggle with telling other people that God is so important He should be first on their daily checklist. An example of my day would be:

CHORES FOR DAY	DONE (CHECK OFF)
Talk to God	
Fix Breakfast	x
Do Laundry	x
Get Kids to School	x
Go to work	x
Talk to God again	
Return from work	x
Take and pick up kids	x
Fix Dinner	x
Talk to God again	
Go to Bed	x

Notice my checkmarks that are missing. That is my normal day. I truly strive for a better relationship and continually feel guilty about not checking off God first in the morning, again in the afternoon, and then again before bed. One morning, my mom sent over a reflection from the Methodist Bishop Mike Coyner. It was just what I needed to read. I want to share that reflection with you because it is core to the understanding of why God should be first and last on your list every day!

"Yes, you do need God" BY BISHOP MICHAEL COYNER

"A new billboard campaign is being launched in central Indiana by a group who wants to promote a secular view of life. They will be placing several large billboards around Indianapolis proclaiming, "You don't need God to hope, to care, to love, to live." One of the persons responsible for this campaign is quoted as saying, "People can live without God. Millions of us do so already. We need to discard once and for all the myth that one needs God in one's life to be a caring, loving person."

Really? Is that true? Do you believe that people can be loving and caring without some kind of religious foundation? I don't see much evidence that it works. Especially over the long run, especially dealing with tough times in life, and especially learning to love people beyond our own family or comfortable circle of friends.

This campaign reinforces the myth in our American culture of 'The Nice Person.' How many times have you heard it said of someone, 'Well, he didn't really go to church or believe in God, but he/she was a nice person'? I have heard that stated at so many funerals, and I have always found it was an excuse to try to celebrate the life of someone who lived in a very narrow circle of caring for family (which is a good thing), being a nice person in social settings (which is OK), but not living much of a life of giving, serving, outreaching, or sacrificing for those beyond that small circle. I have also heard such statements made by family and friends who were totally grief-stricken and unable to deal with the reality of death. By contrast, when I have been a part of funerals for Christian believers, I have found grief and sadness over the loss of a loved one, but it is always coupled with a faith which sustains and enables people to live with hope. Which is why the Apostle Paul says, "We grieve, but not like those who have no hope." Simply being a nice person does not bring much comfort when confronted with the ultimate realities of life and death.

The cultural myth of "The Nice Person" is even more of a fallacy when we examine our lives today. Yes, there are nice people who do lots of nice and benevolent things —

but I don't see much sustaining power for the long-run. Almost anyone can shed a tear over a TV commercial about starving children, maybe even write a check, and then go on with life and believe he/she is a Nice Person. But people who sustain a life-long commitment to caring, sacrifice, sharing with others, and reaching beyond their comfortable circle - those people are almost always people of faith. It is our faith in God, our awareness of being grace-filled people, which enables us to overcome the basic selfishness that confines most people to a life of being just a Nice Person to those who are nice to us.

This "You Don't need God" campaign is an interesting and challenging campaign. It will invite Christians and other God-believers to examine ourselves to make sure we are living our lives in such a way that our faith is clear, caring, hopeful, and joyful. Perhaps this campaign reminds us that we Christians have been very weak in our witness to the power of our faith to move us beyond being "nice people." This campaign is also a sad reminder that so many people today are trying to live their lives without God.

My response is simply this: "Yes, you do need God."

What I find interesting about this article is that God seems to be missing in so many lives, and our society (even our Christian society) is accepting of this. How can I possibly explain to someone what God does for me? From the moment I started penning this book, I knew I needed a chapter on why God must be part of our lives, but I truly struggled with capturing it in the written language. I love that my life is centered upon God (most of the time), and I truly want that for all people, but how can I make those people see that for themselves? The truth is – I cannot do it. God must be part of the picture for me to help guide people to Him.

REVELATIONS 3:15-17 "I know your deeds, that you are neither cold nor hot; I wish that you were cold or hot. So because you are lukewarm, and neither hot nor cold, I will spit you out of My mouth. Because you say, "I am rich, and have become wealthy, and have need of nothing," and you do not know that you are wretched and miserable and poor and blind and naked."

Ouch. Those words are not beating around the bush. Those verses say it plainly. Don't be wish-washy in your faith or God will rebuke you. Don't be a hypocrite about your faith either. Admit you are desperate for God, and then find the richness of your faith, not your wealth.

People with lukewarm belief or no belief are all around us. They are in our neighborhoods, in our schools, in our work places and in our families. They may profess to believe in God, but do not practice it. I am talking about those that do not know the true meaning of sacrifice and servant hood.

These people are desperate for something in their lives that will make them feel special, blessed and wanted. Looking for instantaneous pleasure may start to grow old. Their search will continue in every corner except the corner with God because God makes them admit their mistakes and sins before He will work on their souls. God makes them think deeply about what commitment truly means. God makes them see their true selves, not the one they want people to see. God corners them, and they run off. I know this because I was a lukewarm believer for almost a decade of my life.

During that time in my life, I stayed as far away from church as I could because church was just a confrontation with God. Church was an inconvenience to my schedule. Church can be seen on TV, why do I need to go to church? There are plenty of excuses. I would have done anything to avoid a relationship with God. Actually, I just wanted to avoid God seeing all my sins up close and personal. One of my favorite scapegoats to help explain my non-church affiliation was to focus on the people who go to church every Sunday that were hypocrites and liars. Remember that blame game I talked about earlier? Here is the thing with that; those hypocrites are willing to listen each week to God trying to talk to their souls, and I wasn't. At least they were making an effort. The thought of how prideful I allowed my heart to get during this time in my life makes me cringe just writing this down. I had no idea what I was missing by placing myself first in life instead of placing God first.

The initial step to placing God first is to do something to profess your trust and honor to God. Go to church. (This is where the eye rolling will start). Seriously, church is the best way for God to see that you are trying to dedicate your life to Him. You are not stripped of all your sin because you go to church, but for one hour, you are amongst people who truly believe that living a life according to Christ is worth it. I tell my kids all the time that their friends reflect their own morals. Don't hang around with kids that are making you uncomfortable by their actions. The same goes with adults. If we surround ourselves with friends that have similar or better yet, higher morals, we will become like them. We will strive to be like them.

If you think my idea of church is a little crazy, then check out the bible. Professing your trust in God is shown in the bible with this story (**LUKE CHAPTER 5:1-10**)

Now it happened that while the crowd was pressing around Him and listening to the word of God, He was standing by the lake of Gennesaret; and He saw two boats lying at the edge of the lake; but the fishermen had gotten out of them and were washing their nets. And He got into one of the boats, which was Simon's, and asked him to put out a little way from the land. And He sat down and began teaching the people from the boat. When He had finished speaking, He said to Simon, "Put out into the deep water and let down your nets for a catch." Simon answered and said, "Master, we worked hard all night and caught nothing, but I will do as You say and let down the nets." When they had done this, they enclosed a great quantity of fish, and their nets began to break; so they signaled to their partners in the other boat for them to come and help them. And they came and filled both of the boats, so that they began to sink. But when Simon Peter saw that, he fell down at Jesus' feet, saying, "Go away from me Lord, for I am a sinful man!" For amazement had seized him and all his companions because of the catch of fish which they had taken; and so also were James and John, sons of Zebedee, who were partners with Simon. And Jesus said to Simon, "Do not fear, from now on you will be catching men."

Simon showed his trust in the Lord by placing his net in the water. He knew that they had been fishing all night and had nothing to show for it. He knew the chances of that net being filled were slim to none. He proved his faith in the Lord and lowered that net into the water. It was against all odds. Sometimes God asks us to do things that seem insurmountable. They are unreachable without God there to lead the way.

I cannot help but think of the problem of addiction here. Addiction can be to food, drugs, alcohol, gossip, drama, exercise, control, anxiety, and the list could continue on. Addiction is impossible without God to help us through it. Strong rehabilitation programs recognize that people must reconcile with God in order to fight the battle effectively. By placing our trust in God and allowing Him to work with us– side by side – instead of working alone, we can overcome any obstacle in life. The problem begins when we try to do it all on our own. Humility, pride and selfishness interfere with the process. Just like Simon Peter lowering his net into the water, doing something that we believe is impossible and allowing God to show us how to make it possible can only conquer addiction.

God didn't leave Simon Peter alone to be a "catcher of men." James and John were standing right along with Simon Peter ready to place God first in their lives. They experienced this inspiring moment together and could support each other on this journey. Finding people who truly encourage you and your faith in God is a great way to get your jump start into placing God first. After a church retreat weekend that introduced me to eighteen other women, I found that just by spending time with them, my life became better. My morals were strengthened and blossomed into a wonderful faith filled relationship that I had not experienced before. We start our meetings in prayer, and we find time to thank God for even the struggles that life has thrown at us. Better yet, we support each other through trials, not by negatively reinforcing the problem, but by helping each other see God's light in those trials. Five years after our first weekend together, there are several of us that still meet. We find time to reflect on God's word through scripture and have invited several others to join us. When life throws something at me, I call those women first. Even if we aren't together all the time socially, there is a bond that no one can break between us – it is our faith in God. We found it together, and we will never forget that weekend.

If I weren't open to God, I never would have gone on that weekend and I never would have found those incredible examples of Christ. Their mere friendship has strengthened my relationship with God and encouraged me to strive for God to exist first in my life.

What does all this have to do with evangelization? I think we all evangelize our faith more than we can possibly imagine. When I was at a meeting this past week at church, I asked the question, "If you were to evangelize your relationship with God to a nonbeliever or a lukewarm believer, what would you say that faith does for your own life?" Immediately, the response was, "God gives me hope. When times are tough or when I am struggling, I get through it because I know God has a plan for it all. I am hopeful even in times of turmoil." So, I countered with, "What if you found out that all those lukewarm believers were going to make it to heaven just like you?" The overwhelming response was, "I know that God forgives, but I get so much from dedicating my life to Him now. My life is one filled with hope and unconditional love. I like being God's servant, and it makes my outlook on life and my friendships with others positive and meaningful." So going back to Bishop Mike Coyner's reflection, living a narrow circle of life was not acceptable for the believer. Living life to the fullest was important, and the only way to do that was placing trust in God and experiencing Servanthood firsthand.

This brings me back to the rainbows and thunderstorms. If we live our life under a black cloud that will at any time burst open with storms, how can we possibly find that enjoyable? I believe that God wants us to enjoy life. When I get to heaven, which I hope I do, I know God will cast his judgment on my sins, but I also know if He asks me "Did you enjoy the life I gave you." My response will be "Yes, immensely." Do you know the reason I enjoyed the life He gave me? I delighted in the days that I could stoop down and serve Him. It wasn't that decade of only pleasing my friends or myself. It was the moment that I allowed God back into my life; when my heart broke down and the waters flooded my heart with God's grace.

Study Questions

● CHAPTER EIGHT

01

What does your daily checklist look like? Do you include time to talk with God each day?

02

Reread Bishop Mike Coyner's "Yes, You Do Need God" reflection. Do you know someone that is "A Nice Person" who does lots of great things for others but fails to allow God in his or her life? How would you explain to that person what God does for you? How does God make a difference in your life?

03

Are you a cold, lukewarm or on fire for God believer? What do you strive to be? How can you get to that point?

04

How do you show your trust in God? Do you attend church, do you volunteer, do you allow God to work in you, etc? If you have trouble with this, consider God a friend. How would you explain your friendship?

05

Who is in your support system concerning your faith? What friends allow you to talk freely about God?

06

Can you think of something that is going on at your church or in your life that God may be calling you to experience that would show your trust in Him? Maybe there is a retreat weekend, a ministry, or church service that you have been wavering on that would show your trust in God?

07

Do you live your life under the black cloud of storm (dwelling on the negatives) or under the rainbow of blessings (dwelling on God's plan and what that means to you)? If God were to ask you, "Did you enjoy your life I gave you on earth," What would your answer be?

Acknowledgements.

Sandra Burdick, God Is No Stranger (Durham:Light Messages, 2004), 24.

Thomas A. Kempis, Imitation of Christ (New York: Catholic Book Publishing Corp, 1993), 15.

Elaine N. Aron, PH.D., The Highly Sensitive Child (New York: Broadway Books, 2002), 117-119.

Max Lucado, Grace for the Moment (Nashville, TN: J. Countryman, 2000), 67.

Tony Dungy with Nathan Whitaker, Quite Strength (Carol Stream, Illinois: Tydale House Publishers, Inc, 2007), 38-39.

Thomas A. Kempis, Imitation of Christ (New York: Catholic Book Publishing Corp, 1993), 15.

Max Lucado, God Came Near (Nashville, TN: Thomas Nelson, 1986, 2004), 85.

Mother Teresa of Calcutta. www.catholicbible101.com/motherteresaquotes.htm

www.catholicbible101.com/motherteresaquotes.htm. Catholicbible101, 2008

Aha! Jokes, www.AhaJokes.com

James C. Hunter, The Servant, A Simple Story About the Ture Essence of Leadership (New York: Crown Business, 1998), 54.

Joel Osteen Ministries. Victoria Osteen. www.joelosteen.com/Hope
ForToday/ThoughtsOn/Family/curtainoffear/Pages/curtainoffear.aspx

Fr. Eamon Tobin, Ascension Catholic Press. www.ascensioncatholic.net/
catechism/catechism_10.pdf

Sandra Burdick, God Is No Stranger (Durham:Light Messages, 2004), 24

Joanna Weaver, Having a Mary Spirit (Colorado Springs: WaterBrook Press,
2006), 153.

Indiana Conference, The United Methodist Church. Bishop Mike Coyner.
http://inumc.org/epistles/detail/43493

The Servant Song. Composed and written by Richard Gillard.

www.MakingRoomForGod.com

MAKING

ROOM FOR

G.com D